Oxford Studies in Education

Children Using Mathematics

**The Mathematics Section of the Association of Teachers
in Colleges and Departments of Education**

Editors: **K.L. Gardner**—*Brighton College of Education*
           J.A. Glenn—*Kesteven College of Education*
           A.I.G. Renton—*Ripon College of Education*

Oxford University Press 1973

Oxford University Press, Ely House, London W. 1

GLASGOW NEW YORK TORONTO MELBOURNE WELLINGTON
CAPE TOWN IBADAN NAIROBI DAR ES SALAAM LUSAKA ADDIS ABABA
DELHI BOMBAY CALCUTTA MADRAS KARACHI LAHORE DACCA
KUALA LUMPUR SINGAPORE HONG KONG TOKYO

Printed in Great Britain by
Fletcher and Sons. Ltd. Norwich

CONTENTS

INTRODUCTION

This report results from a conference on the theme 'Progression in Primary Mathematics' held at Homerton College, Cambridge, in September 1970. It was organized jointly by the Department of Education and Science and the Association of Teachers in Colleges and Departments of Education.

The report is not an account of 'modern mathematics' but attempts to discuss aspects of primary teaching in a way that will help those who have to plan the activities of the classroom. As originally drafted it included a typical work-scheme which fitted the recommendations of the report, but this was removed at a later stage as we felt that it might be taken as a new gospel rather than an illustration.

Since the impetus of primary work rests on the skills and knowledge of the teacher we must be deeply concerned with the mathematical backgrounds both of the young entrant leaving his Department or College of Education and of the established teacher whose own training came before the new approaches to content and method. The Association, therefore, began an independent survey among a group of some fifty experienced teachers to establish what in their view was an optimum syllabus for professional training in mathematics. The findings of this survey are incorporated with the Homerton discussions on the same topic in the appendix to this report.

The Association is grateful to Mr. Ian Butterworth, H.M.I. of the Department of Education and Science for his help and support in the task of organizing the conference. The Department is not, of course, in any way responsible for the views we have expressed.

The material from the conference has been edited on behalf of the A.T.C.D.E. Mathematics Section by

K.L. Gardner	—	Brighton College of Education
J.A. Glenn	—	Kesteven College of Education
A.I.G. Renton	—	Ripon College of Education

The Association is indebted to Mrs. I.M. Carrott for her patience and skill in typing the successive drafts of the report.

CHAPTER ONE

THE APPROACH TO MATHEMATICS TEACHING

Thomas Hobbes said 'Words are wise men's counters, they do but reckon with them'. In discussing mathematics we are concerned with words and with the multitude of ideas behind them. We are concerned with development from these ideas both mathematically and pedagogically. We are especially concerned with the rates of change in the significance of words, algorithms, ideas.

If we only look back as far as the birth date of the majority of our current school leavers, we find the report of the Mathematical Association, *The teaching of algebra in Sixth Forms* (1957) looking warily at the changes then appearing and saying: 'As a general rule school teaching should not be in a hurry to adapt itself to new trends in the more advanced parts of mathematics'. Only five years later the same Association noted in *A review of new trends in Mathematical Education at the Secondary Stage* that with the teaching of mathematics as an important interest, a Curriculum Study Group had been set up within the Ministry of Education 'at a time characterized above all by the speed of change'. This review also described the initiation of the School Mathematics Project with the announcement that 'an imaginative pilot scheme will require the production of textbooks from an up-to-date point of view to correspond to the new curricula'. However, the veil of caution still thrown at that time over any spontaneous work of an unfamiliar nature was well shown by the concluding paragraph on 'Putting theory into practice', viz: 'With regard to the teaching of mathematics the Nuffield Foundation is still at an exploratory stage in its thinking. It is understood that it will seek to support and strengthen work already in progress rather than initiate new activities of its own and, in view of the promising pioneer work already being organized, this is surely a policy to be welcomed.'

The policy of supporting rather than initiating new moves was welcomed at the time by some. To see the performance in retrospect a decade later, one need only step inside one of the Teachers' Centres (many of them set up at the suggestion of the Nuffield Mathematics

Project). One can then appreciate some of the pioneer work and new activities generated in Primary schools, as well as the tremendous extent to which the work already in progress has been encouraged and strengthened. It is utterly impossible to itemize all souces from which sprang a new attitude to the life and work of children in schools: many tiny eruptions of dissatisfaction with the current system had occurred and many working parties had made their own small marks on the scholastic tally stick by the time the now familiar pilot schemes began operating in various regions. These were perhaps reflections of the significant changes in outlook of the whole of our society. At the upper end of the scale there was the dissatisfaction of the universities with the number and quality of the students coming forward for specialized study, together with the growing need of industrialists to use and to understand the possibilities of mathematics in many situations previously thought immune to such abstract ideas.

Business men began to expect young mathematicians entering their organizations to be able to set up mathematical models from which management could 'read off' the answers to some of their major decision problems. This demanded not only traditional facility in handling techniques, but also far deeper insight into both the possibilities and the limitations not only of the mathematical situations but the industrial ones as well.

Traditional mathematical training left many young employees sadly floundering, and demand grew for a renewed element of imaginative creativity to be developed in mathematical teaching.

We do not dwell in this report on the particular needs of business, industry, and technology; but the question of regarding mathematics as a creative activity brings us right into the classroom situation at all levels, so also do other threads being strongly woven into the sociological pattern. Notable among these is the tremendous increase in use of mathematical forms and language, growing towards more useful, concise, economical and increasingly normal modes of expression. Closely related to this is the almost incredible surge in commercial production of all kinds of apparatus for school use, particularly of a scientific and mathematical nature. While appreciating the very obvious advantages of the availability of this material, we can see that there are the same dangers of 'authority' in catalogued material as in the printed word, and the very opportunities offered simultaneously create their own problems of choice and use.

Nor are these difficulties decreased by yet another strand of development. The teacher is being increasingly bombarded by reports of psychological or educational experiments purporting to show that this or that approach will do less good or more good than accustomed methods, and will ease his burden of responsibility for the learning of the class in his charge (still as a rule far too large in number). We discuss below what we regard as the most important of these ideas and experiments, but note here that these are increasingly being reported directly to the teacher and the public. The pressure of events is tending to bypass interpretation by educational theorists and more and more fresh and effective approaches to mathematics are arising from spontaneous generation in the classroom. Close co-operation between the teachers, the local advisers, and lecturers in Colleges of Education thus becomes essential. We must extend into varied situations the best achievements of individuals in particular circumstances, mould general theories to fit a certain group of children, and evaluate our efforts effectively. Without this cooperation in evaluation we run the danger on the one hand of offering the children the shell of an idea without its kernel and on the other the lack of realism so often pointed out by the warning finger raised to educational theorists.

Corresponding to changes in the outlook of both society and the educationalists, the raw material of the educational system is changing too. Although it is still true that children will always be children, and that certain factors of their growth and development remain constant, yet the environment is so vastly different that today's Reception Class would hardly be recognized as the starting point of school life by the teacher of a generation or so ago. True, there are still many children who arrive for their first day at school lacking important experiences and without desirable social training (it is not to be expected that they can all perform difficult tasks like tying shoe laces), but the majority have already ingested quantities of technical knowledge and have absorbed information on a wide range of topics from television and elsewhere. That the technological background of infant school children may already outstrip that of their teacher within certain fields adds to her difficulties in coping with the immense diversity of problems she still has to face. It demands understanding and organizing ability of a high order.

A uniform social background scarcely exists, and the teacher has to weld into working groups a large collection of very varied individuals, the majority of whom will not be able for a long time to read instructions or write down observations. How can she possibly discover the extent and depth of their abilities to cope with the wealth of early mathematical ideas, find their separate weaknesses and provide for continuing progress at these vital stages? Let us take a more detailed look at one of the concepts usually tackled early, the learning of measurement. We choose to refer to length, as this is generally regarded as the most convenient type of quantity to approach first. In choosing it we want it to be understood that we are only using it as an example of the background of understanding called for by the common classroom topics. We shall use it again later.

Here a prerequisite for the young child is the ability to discriminate between discrete and continuous substances. Since a quantity consists of a number and a unit, to measure a quantity units are stepped out until the requisite size is achieved and so the measure is quantified. Thus, in order to measure some quantity, a young child must learn four things. He must realize that in abstracting one property, say length, all other qualities (e.g. colour, texture, weight, cross section) are of no concern. He must learn to repeat units and count: the one–one correspondence between the number names and the objects being counted is far more important than the ability to recite the jingle, and herein lie difficulties enough, some of which we consider later. Further, the young child must be given the opportunity to mix up different sizes of units, to find that the results are not meaningful and to realize—it is by no means obvious to five- and six-year olds—that he must repeat *equal* units. Then he must learn that there must be no gaps in spacing the units along the item to be measured, and also no overlaps—even ten-year olds can be seen doing remarkable things with rulers or metre sticks in playground and hall through failure to recognize this fact!

Beyond these, to make intelligent use of measurement the child must also come to appreciate:

1. That measurements of length are unchanged by time or by sliding, turning, raising or lowering, colouring or folding. Folding, of course,

alters the distance between the ends, but does not change the actual length. The conservation of length must be treated with respect. If the teacher has not as an adult looked at, say, the mast of a dinghy lying on the ground as compared with its upright position aboard, such an experience is to be recommended as very salutary. Moreover, conservation fails in some cases under processes like washing, heating, pulling, or squeezing. The concept is by no means simple.

2. That units must be stated for a measurement to be meaningful: a mere number does not give a quantity.

3. That units need to be communicable, i.e. we need standard units which are invariant under changes of time, place, operator, etc.

4. That smaller units will need more of them as compared with the same quantity measured in fewer, larger units—this is a vital concept for coping with conversions later and for the sensible choice of a unit of measurement to keep the number of units reasonable. To decide what is reasonable is frequently a difficult exercise anyway.

Further, for measurement of length in particular, the child needs to appreciate:

5. That it is symmetric—the distance from home to school is the same as that from school to home, one-way streets permitting.

6. That measurement of distance has two aspects. There is distance along a given route or path, and distance as the crow flies. If one is measuring an object one has to decide whether or not it is the overall length that is needed.

7. That the distance to a wall, for example, is the perpendicular distance, however this is presented to the child.

8. That in practice, when measuring length the first unit may be removed when each adjacent one is positioned, but not before, so one can indeed use just one copy of the unit, as long as the end spot is marked for the beginning of the next placing. This is again not at all obvious to six-year olds.

9. That if we wish to compare a set of measurements, they must all be taken in the same or convertible units. This is another concept in its own right.

So the teacher of young children learning about measurement needs to offer them equipment and give them the situational freedom which does not prohibit mistakes in all the aspects detailed above. Not all children need to make all the mistakes, though many more than at present should have the opportunity to do so, with the result that the pupils really come to see what does not work and achieve understanding of the principles involved. Only such understanding enables them in due course to apply the principles in other situations and to see whether or not different situations require different approaches.

Without doubt the above quite sophisticated topic, which is only one of several major ones attempted in the mathematics of the early years of primary education, is enough to keep Infants and Lower Juniors busy for many hours! From the point of view of the teacher utilizing or devizing appropriate situations, work on any topic must be welded into that of the whole day for each child, and for the whole class for the term and year. The teacher has, so to speak, a preview of the results she expects with regard to the child's learning and, while pursuing activities aimed perhaps primarily at developing ideas of length, the teacher may well be using such material for other purposes. She may be using it to extend the pupils' knowledge, say, of colour, or in connection with some creative activity. To the child the activity is something interesting to do—it must appear relevant to *him* at *that* moment in time, and cannot be pushed further than *he* is able to go just then, as—unlike the teacher—he cannot yet know where the work is really leading. The teacher on the other hand should be aware of approaches likely to be adopted and may encourage the child to try a variety of these, but she must avoid being too dogmatic or her very help may stifle the germination of thought in the child's mind rather than encourage its development. Thus the adult member of this working partnership needs to analyze the real importance of any activity or experiment so that she can help to clarify progress along various lines. She must distinguish between the child's temporary conclusions soon to be absorbed or even jettisoned in favour of deeper ideas and the more abiding and funda-mental realizations.

Clearly the demands made on the teacher are almost unlimited. She must not only have considerable understanding of the foundations of mathematical thinking and learning and the inter-relations of its differ-ent aspects, but also she must be able to cope similarly with the vital early stages of language work, movement, creative activities, music, and all the rest. She is expected to recognize growing points in all these areas and to lead perhaps forty or more youngsters through this maze in steady growth.

So we are brought up against two apparently conflicting requirements for the teacher—the depth of specialized knowledge on the one hand and the width of experience and broad array of subject matter to be covered on the other—and each of these requirements today goes far beyond the bounds set in most schools even as late as the middle of this century.

To try and meet these requirements we are seeing today immensely widespread discussions and experiments on reorganization of initial training opportunities, with developments in contacts for teacher with teacher even across the boundaries of pupil age groups. We do not in this report deal with changes in organization and administration within Colleges of Education or other initial training systems, but we do reflect the development of thinking within Colleges who are adjusting their work to correspond to the new freedom of approach in today's classrooms. Both teachers in training and children in school are being increasingly encouraged to carry over to their mathematics ideas and situations occurring in other contexts of life and work. We are beginning to see lecturers in departments of, say, art and mathematics discussing together topics like curve stitching, the construction of solids, or notions of similarity and symmetry. The basic ideas of these emerge, freed from restraints of precision and varied with colour, texture, and medium, in painting and embroidery. Yet another look can be provided by music and movement, where dance forms can follow mathematical patterns so that in the primary classroom we may see children painting mathematical shapes and symmetrical patterns, tracing shapes with their bodies in Physical Education, recording rhythm patterns and musical notes in mathematical forms, making models both of realistic and abstract forms, making tables, flowcharts, and mapping diagrams to record their information on the project currently in hand. An interesting example recently seen grew from a Reception Class's interest in colours. After Physical Education one day they sorted themselves into sets according to the colours of their shoes, formed a circle in the room round a centre marker, put radii of cords to separate the sets arranged in arcs, and compared the sizes of the sectors with the numbers of people and shoes in the sets and with the whole class, the whole circle.

All then drew round their shoes, labelled them and put them in the appropriate sector with the name of the colours written round the circumference. A valuable amount of language work evolved and many growing points emerged from this simple situation, in which the basic ideas of a pie-chart were introduced without any of the complications of measuring angles or knowing about degrees. Finally, 'what it looks like' and 'what it says' was discussed in comparison with other representations of the same information. It is in this way that the background to topic teaching is expanded.

An increasingly familiar example of a similar approach is through cooking activities where aspects of time, money, temperature, capacity, volume, and number (with re-arrangements of the items counted) all occur. There is also a considerable element of social education both from cooperation in learning and from taking responsibility on behalf of the group. Many teachers find these very satisfying and stimulating activities, provided the work has been properly organized and space and help are available. Working on the pattern of an integrated day, allowing set points for activities for which facilities must be shared, suits the modern view of learning. In spite of presenting its own problems, it seems to be a type of organization which once tried is not willingly abandoned. The use of the integrated day often accompanies family grouping with a two-to-three-year age range in a class. If this arrangement is being adopted for the first time, children already used to a more rigid timetable need time to adapt to the freer conditions. Perhaps a partial changeover paving the way is better than a sudden abandonment of the familiar routine. However, it is generally found that there is little problem in achieving an adequate range of work and breadth of experience, and that the youngsters thrive on the opportunity to pursue an activity without undue interruption. They move quite naturally to a complementary type of activity at a suitable point for the changeover. One essential requirement for the teacher, however, is to keep track of the children's progress along various lines of development. This is not primarily for her own needs: the extent to which teachers of young children know in detail just what each of the forty-plus children in their care has so far achieved is almost unbelievable to anyone not closely in touch with their work. But there are many circumstances, such as the illness of a teacher or a change of home locality, which render it necessary to be able to report on the work a child has done at that point. The form that such a report should take is currently under discussion in many areas of the country, and is closely tied up with the whole question of assessment, which we discuss below in Chapter 9. In mathematics, it is now clear that the logic of a child's learning is of a quite different order from that of an adult rationally organizing abstract ideas in retrospect. Besides this, it is impossible to know with any degree of certainty what factors have been the objects of a child's attention mentally and emotionally, so that one cannot be sure even what pieces of the total jig-saw puzzle picture are being handled. We can be even less sure to what extent the pieces have appeared to the child to fit together. Too careful presentation by the teacher in the order she sees as appropriate may perhaps inhibit the association for the child. This is a dilemma, and teaching is indeed an art transcending a mere skill! An increasing number of primary schools are extending the idea of a class topic to one adopted by several classes, or perhaps even by the whole school. Under the umbrella of this topic a great many aspects are considered simultaneously, and interplay between groups of children working with different adults enables gaps in experience to be filled. A wide variety of expertise may be available to help any individual child and stimulate his efforts, improving motivation for discussion and careful presentation reporting back to the group. The importance of crystallizing ideas from an early age in words, diagrams, tables, and flowcharts cannot be overstressed as helping the development of the growing notions of the child and these also reveal to the teachers the stages reached, the misconceptions or partial understandings, particular interests, or individual flairs and talents. We note, too, the different roles played by discussion on the one hand between child and child, where neither is the authority, and between child and teacher. Opinions are often upheld tenaciously in the one case, but relinquished easily in the other. With good personal relationship the gap will close, but the teacher still has a distinct role to play since the more the child respects her, the more weight her suggestions will carry. The danger of stifling creativity by imposing ideas or methods always exists, but may be reduced by the habit of offering several suggestions from which one or none may be chosen. At the same time the drive to ensure progression, or even the desire to get something good for display on the walls, may easily lead from the essential minimum to an over-riding maximum of help. The balance is very fine, but perhaps realization of the delicacy of the situation is the best guard against a foolish rushing in 'where angels fear to tread'. Young teachers are often helped by the internal discussions of a school staff, especially where there is a class teacher specialist. This is perhaps of great importance for mathematics, where the heart of the matter, the abstract idea, has to be inferred from the situation. Rather than being explicitly recorded or displayed it is implicit in particular examples given or diagrams drawn. We suggest later that the nature of mathematics may demand more specific skills than can emerge from a completely undifferentiated timetable. Further ideas and inspiration will certainly be generated through in-service training. This training may be informal through *ad hoc* meetings in a Teachers' Centre, through regular discussion groups, or more closely organized in courses. It will be particularly important in discussing the possibilities of new apparatus, the availability of equipment, and the use or adaption of familiar material. As pressures increase, surely the secondment of teachers for suitable courses of study will need to be considered, with staff allocations allowing for teachers to be freed in rotation. This seems implied by the demands for increased knowledge and experience over the whole range of topics arising in the primary classroom. Only by such means can we be sure that the over-hesitant teacher will receive the chance of re-inforcement, and the over-confident teacher be brought to think again. All should have the opportunity of sharing more widely both their problems and their successes. One person's success is another's inspiration. We must not forget that teachers need, just as the children do, the opportunity to crystallize thinking by discussion and exchange. They too need stimulation and encouragement.

CHAPTER TWO

TEACHING STRATEGIES APPROPRIATE TO PRIMARY SCHOOL MATHEMATICS

This chapter discusses strategies which may be employed in the teaching of primary mathematics. We examine the nature of mathematics, the development of the child, and the reasons for teaching mathematics. We then consider some of the more recent ideas which have come to us from educationists and psychologists and endeavour to interpret them in our context. There are many new ideas in primary mathematics and most have some merit. Our aims are to locate the basic features of these and to give teachers the opportunity to fit them into a practical scheme of teaching.

2.1 What is mathematics?

Many definitions of mathematics are either too narrow to be comprehensive or too wide to be of value, but we can argue that almost every area of human investigation needs at some stage to consider such attributes as quantity, order, or structure. It is, therefore, reasonable and economical to study these attributes as a separate discipline, and this study, suitably abstracted, is known as mathematics.

From the above definition the basic characteristics of mathematics may readily be derived. In spite of recent developments in primary schools mathematics is still basically an abstract subject, since the elements which it manipulates are themselves abstract—'three' cannot exist concretely except as three apples or three desks. Mathematics is also precise and ordered since its fundamentals themselves have that quality. These characteristics are what makes mathematics difficult but rewarding both to teach and to learn.

The proud claim that mathematics is 'the queen of the arts and the handmaid of science' may need re-expression today, but it is clear that ever-increasing areas of human thought and activity are being explored with the aid of mathematics. The distinction between a descriptive and an exact science is precisely one of mathematical formulation, and we see sciences such as sociology entering the ranks of quantitative studies. What risks they face in payment is not for this report to decide. The 'handmaid' aspect is clear enough, since most scientists at some time or other call on their mathematical colleagues for help or guidance with specific problems. Mathematics itself however, transcends this limited role: it is not merely a part of environmental science or a theme on British Rail. It can serve such activities and play a major part in producing organized and well disciplined studies, but these activities have little to do with the basic nature of mathematics.

Mathematics deals with such topics as quantity, order, pattern, and structure wherever these may appear. It may be used as a powerful weapon in the investigation of other subjects or themes but by its very nature transcends these and should not be limited in this way.

2.2   Mathematics in action

Our next step is to investigate mathematicians in action. Let us consider the stages followed in solving a problem. The four stages are simplified here and the reader is referred to Hadamard [1] for a more detailed analysis:

1. A period of intensive hard work when the problem is pulled to pieces and examined from various points of view.
2. A pause during which, apparently, some form of unconscious mental processing takes place which results in:
3. The moment of discovery when the solution appears as it were out of the blue, and often at a most unlikely moment.
4. The final period of hard work after the breakthrough when the full solution is produced and verified.

These four stages are condensed in the final results to theorems derived by explicit logical arguments from the initial assumptions. Readers may have met this approach in the Euclidean Geometry they learned at secondary school and may well have had their views of mathematics and mathematicians distorted as a result.

The final solution to a problem must, in the end, be precise. Otherwise, the mathematician's colleagues cannot rely on his results, and the engineer's bridge will fall down or the astronaut's rocket will miss the moon. Yet traditional teaching in primary schools has tended to emphasize precision and accuracy in arithmetic often to the exclusion of the more exciting aspects of the subject. Precision, accuracy, and competence there must be, but this is by no means the whole story.

Human beings are not precise and accurate in all their works. They are naturally prone to error and indeed error is part of the process of discovery. In teaching we should learn to take advantage of errors, and not simply aim to eradicate them.

As far as the subconscious creative stages are concerned, there is little that we can do except to provide the circumstances in which they can happen. The creative processes may be encouraged to work by providing situations in which a child will become seriously involved. Without the basic motivation, the tensions apparently necessary for creative effort will not develop and neither will the joy and satisfaction at the release of tension occasioned by the final solution. The problems children tackle must be such as to motivate them sufficiently highly to allow the creative processes to operate if this be at all possible.

The moment of discovery is not to be confused with the use of those discovery methods in teaching mathematics which have been so admirably championed by H.M. Inspector Miss Edith Biggs and others over the last ten years. We will return to these later. Clearly discovery methods are closely linked with out present topic but what we are concerned with here is the natural discovery which is an integral part of mathematical activity, and which is independent of the methods of teaching employed. Discovery methods have, quite rightly, sought to capitalize on this vital, but often neglected, aspect of mathematical activity.

We have now derived the following implications for the teaching of mathematics:

1. Mathematicians in action tend to think in the same way as other creative workers. There is an emphasis in their work, however, on precision, accuracy, and competence and the very definite need for the verification of results.
2. Problem situations for children must be child-centred to give the the maximum motivation and involvement so that a child's creative ability should have full opportunity to act.
3. Discovery is a natural part of mathematical activity and inherent in the solution of all mathematical problems, however they are pre-

sented. Mathematical discovery is satisfying and strongly motivating.

An example at primary level will demonstrate the validity of the approach.

A group of children are investigating the graphical properties of the 2-times table and are beginning to produce the graph of Fig. 1. It is

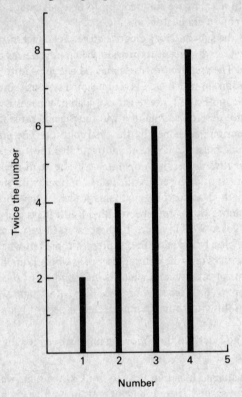

Figure 1

assumed that they are fully involved in this exercise and anxious to reach their conclusions. The first need here is for precision, for if 2 × 3 is taken as 5, the whole solution falls to pieces. The situation is straight-forward and a child rapidly reaches the conclusion that all the numbers lie on a line. This is a useful discovery based on four number facts but it does need to be verified. A ruler will help us check that the four values

given do in fact lie on a line and that the remaining products up to
12 × 2 = 24 and even beyond may also be shown to fit. Thus the children have plotted their graph precisely and with accurate figures, made
their discovery, and verified within their own limits.

We may extend the example by further abstraction. The problem is
abstract in its own right, since the 2-times table is itself an abstraction.
The fact that the points lie on a straight line may be abstracted from the
situation and the general rule discovered for any multiplication table.
With bright children and good luck we may abstract rather differently
and investigate whether any line through the origin can in fact represent
a multiplication table. This can lead to further generalizations with such
interesting phenomena as the 1½-times table!

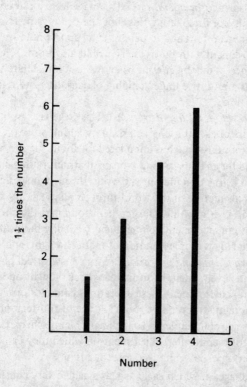

Figure 2

All the above is good mathematics and can help to establish even at the primary stage the pattern of thought we require.

2.3   Development psychology

Through the now familiar works of Jean Piaget and his associates, we know that a child's mental growth is a continuous process from birth and that his thought processes are by no means those of an adult. The developmental variable is a vital one in the teaching of mathematics to primary children. So that we shall be able to build this into our strategies, it is necessary to outline the stages of cognitive development which Piaget claims.

Stage 1 : Sensori-motor operations   This stage lasts for about the first eighteen months of life. During this time the child learns to coordinate actions with perceptions and to behave in an appropriate way, such as following movement with the eyes. The child also learns to appreciate the permanence of an object even when it is not immediately before him and gains a primitive understanding of causation and relationships in space and time.

Stage 2 : Concrete thinking operations   This stage lasts until about eleven or twelve years of age. It is characterized by a long process of elaboration of mental operations, which is completed by about the age of seven and is then followed by an equally long process of structuration. In the first part the child learns to represent the world through images and words. He organizes his picture of the world through play, talking, questioning, listening, and experimenting. During the second part the child learns to cope with his immediate environment and gradually builds up, at first intuitively, the ideas of conservation of matter, weight, and dimensions.

Stage 3 : Formal thinking operations   Stage 3 is abstract and characterized by the development of formal, abstract thought operations. In a rich, cultural environment these operations come to form a stable system of thought structures at about the age of fourteen or fifteen. During this stage children learn to tackle problems schematically and come to perform controlled experiments in which they can observe the effect of altering one or more variables at a time.

The actual ages at which each stage is attained vary considerably from child to child and there is no clear borderline between the end of one stage and the beginning of the next. What is important, however, is that Piaget considers that the order in which the stages appear is fixed and this does provide us with a framework against which we can examine our teaching. Piaget's thoughts have been so much with us that it is now difficult to find any area in the primary field which has not been influenced by him. The following lines of argument, however, do seem to stem directly from his researches.

Children in the primary school are in the 'concrete thinking' stage (two to eleven). Thus, even at the top end of the junior school, children may well have difficulty in hypothetical reasoning and would feel happiest when thinking with objects. We must, however, be fair about this. Many adults feel exactly the same way. The implications are clear. The mathematics done in primary schools must be geared to practical activities if it is to be at a cognitive level which the child can understand. Thus we may justify the tendency to convert mathematics in the primary schools to a practical subject. This has taken a variety of forms: the apparently random collecting of old junk, the use of plentiful supplies of straws, pipecleaners, cardboard, and paste, to more sophisticated physical experiments such as toy trains rolling down slopes. But however successful the theory, the practice is fraught with difficulty. A child sorting through a pile of old junk may be gaining valuable experience in classification and elementary set theory. On the other hand, he may not. We must also remember that even if primary mathematics is now to a considerable extent a practical subject, mathematics itself is basically abstract. Primary teachers need to look beyond the primary school if they are to do the best they can for their pupils. The inner principles demonstrated by any situation need to be brought out by class discussion.

The previous paragraph deals with primary children in general but Piaget's work is more precise than this. Within a class of forty children of much the same age, there will be considerable differences in cognitive development and work suitable for one child will be by no means suitable for his neighbour. This leads us to an approach where work for each child needs to be geared to his own level if frustration both on the part of the teacher and the pupil is to be avoided. An example will perhaps clarify this. We know it is possible for a child faced with a pile of sweets on a desk to be able to count them accurately, but to consider that there are more when the sweets are spread out over the desk. Recent experiments have shown that the young child finds the concept 'more than' ambiguous in such a situation. He may say there are 'more' because they cover more surface, even if the wording of the question implies for us a strict numerical comparison, but in any case it is clear from his reactions that he finds this situation difficult to handle. His neighbour, on the other hand, finds the task trivial and beneath contempt. This is clear from his reactions also. Certainly the first child needs more experience to develop either his number concepts, or his knowledge of their application. The second child is past this stage and is ready for simple arithmetic. What, however, can

$$5 \text{ sweets} + 3 \text{ sweets} = 8 \text{ sweets}$$

mean if the sweets alter in quantity as you move them round the desk, or if you do not realize that it is their number which is being discussed? Granted the general truth of Piaget's conclusions, a child-centred approach is the most effective method, but this is not to give a *carte-blanche* to more extreme forms of child-centred learning.

The need for work to be geared to the cognitive level of the child follows logically from Piaget's work. What is more difficult is to establish this as a practical proposition. To this end, the Nuffield Mathematics Project and Piaget and his associates have combined and produced the Nuffield Guides *Checking Up*, *1* and *2* [2], which are designed to transform this aspect of Piaget's work into a useful tool. The initial drafts presented difficulties, but we hope that these have been ironed out and that the final versions will fully justify their illustrious parenthood. The film *Checking Up* provides useful evidence of this approach in action.

2.4 Why learn mathematics?

We have outlined what mathematics is about, how mathematicians think, and how children develop mathematical concepts. We now consider why children should learn mathematics.

1. *Mathematics for living* This term refers to those aspects of mathematics which an individual must know in order to function adequately as a member of society. At primary level this clearly includes such topics as number, time, money, length, and weight. These must be

with us in modern or traditional syllabuses and justify themselves even to the most eccentric curriculum reformer. It is difficult, however, to know when to stop. More and more information is presented in statistical form and this trend will continue. The educated person must be able to evaluate such data effectively if he is to play a full and useful part in society. Most people will, at some time or other, be involved with such complex activities as house purchase, hire purchase, and insurance. An educated person should understand these things. Some of the problems raised here are more noticeable at secondary level. It is, for example, notoriously difficult to interest fifteen-year olds in the arithmetic of mortgages and life insurance, but somehow or other the schools *must* equip their pupils to deal with these social calculations.

2. *Mathematics for vocation* This follows naturally from the previous section and deals with those aspects of mathematics which are required for specific jobs. It need not concern us unduly here since it is largely the province of the technical side of higher education. We must emphasize, however, that, with the increasing use of mathematical techniques in all areas of human endeavour, more and more people will find themselves in need of this aspect of mathematical training. Thus mathematical education in schools, although not specifically vocational, must leave children in a position to make the best use of their opportunities.

3. *Mathematics for education* It is one of the functions of the educational philosopher to meditate on the nature, purpose, and content of education. A recent contribution from Professors Hirst and Peters [3] isolates seven modes of knowledge and experience, distinguished by a particular type of concept. Their list is as follows:

(a) *Formal logic and mathematics*—involving concepts of a general abstract kind.
(b) *Physical sciences*—eventually involved with knowledge of the sensible world.
(c) *"Knowledge without observation"*—involving terms such as believing, deciding, hoping, and enjoying.
(d) *Moral judgement and awareness*—involving expressions such as ought, wrong, or duty.
(e) *Aesthetic experience*—involving *inter alia* non-linguistic forms of symbolic expression.

(f) *Religion*—involving such concepts as divinity.
(g) *Philosophy*—with unique second-order concepts irreducible to any of those mentioned above.

It is claimed that these seven modes are based on clearly distinguishable cognitive structures; that each involves a distinctive form of reasoning and judgement. Although some readers may deny the usefulness or even the validity of such a division, it is true that on the basis of this or a similar list we may argue that education should involve all categories of knowledge and experience, so that mathematics has a necessary and prominent part to play.

4. *Mathematics for civilization* It may be argued that the aesthetic, affective aspects of human endeavour, are of primary importance in children's education, as they are in civilization.

Mathematics has its own place in the history of thought. The citizen of ancient Greece admired philosophy, music, and mathematics. A knowledge of Euclid was a necessity for a cultured Renaissance man, and Dante used metaphors from geometry as freely as the Victorians did from horticulture. Throughout the ages in the major civilizations, a knowledge of mathematics has been as much the mark of education as a knowledge of the visual arts.

The aesthetic side of mathematics is more difficult to explain, again because of its abstract nature. Mathematics is, or should be, a creative subject with the emotional satisfaction inherent in any creative exercise. Since it is unrestricted by the limitations of paint or stone, however, it can achieve a level of formal perfection in general beyond the reach of more physical arts. We may thus justify the teaching of mathematics on social, vocational, philosophical, and cultural grounds, and each of these indicate different aims and objectives for the learning process.

We have suggested four ways of looking at mathematics, and we now consider what type of content they produce and the aims and objectives they require.

Mathematics for living This is the most straightforward to analyze. Its content is chosen on the basis of the practical needs of an educated person. Much of it, like telling the time, consists of techniques which give us a set of readily testable objectives. To make the best use of these techniques, such 'concepts' as time should be 'understood', accepting for the moment the imprecision of the terms in inverted commas. Finally, the children's attitude towards mathematics should be a positive one in that they are prepared to use the mathematics they have learnt.

Mathematics for vocation   This is not directly the concern of the primary school, but we must leave children in a position to make the best use of opportunities later on. Although the content has not the immediate relevance to the outside world of 'Mathematics for living', precision and technical competence are still of importance because of the basic nature of mathematics. Children must learn to think mathematically in practical situations and to enjoy doing so.

Mathematics for education: Here we considered mathematics as one of the seven modes of knowledge or experience. Much of the content in this field is too sophisticated for primary children, but we would certainly include such topics as basic work on sets and relations under this heading as providing techniques for the establishment of pattern and order in confused situations.

Mathematics for civilization: The emphasis changes considerably here, and this aspect is frequently lost under the deluge of more prosaic needs. Choice of content is of less importance here but should reflect an intellectual need, have some historical significance, or be there because it is enjoyable in its own right. The emphasis would tend to be on the creative aspects of mathematics.

2.5   Teaching strategies

1.   *Summary to date*   In this section we attempt to capitalize on all that has gone before and begin by summarizing earlier sections.

(a)   We emphasized the special qualities of abstraction and precision in all mathematics, but noted its applicability to almost every other subject or topic.

(b)   We discussed the creative, discovery aspects of mathematics and the need for problem situations of sufficient interest to stimulate the creative faculty. We noted the need for precision and verification.

(c)   Our account of mental development indicated the need for practical work and a child-centred approach.

(d)   We then gave reasons for the teaching of mathematics under the headings of mathematics for living, for vocation, for education and for civilization.

(e) We summarized our aims as establishing a positive attitude to mathematics, so that children could think mathematically, learn techniques, and gain an understanding of concepts.

2. *Structures of content* If we break down content into a series of concepts and techniques and the relations between them, it becomes apparent that certain topics cannot be learnt until others have been mastered. This gives us a logical hierarchy of topics. An example will make this clear.

Suppose we wish to teach simple addition of the form

$$\begin{array}{r} 23 \\ + 18 \\ \hline 41 \end{array}$$

If this is to be learned with full understanding, then the following major concepts and techniques at least would need to be learnt beforehand.

(a) The concept of place value
(b) Simple number facts
(c) The concept of number

Each of the two concepts involved, however, are themselves capable of further analysis. For example, the concept of number itself may be broken down further into conservation of number, knowledge of number-names, and one—one correspondence. Thus a child is not ready to tackle simple addition of the type shown until he has reached the development stage where he realizes that a set has a fixed number of elements (conservation), can match these elements with the appropriate subset of number names, knows his simple number facts and has some understanding of addition and place value. These last two concepts themselves may and should be analyzed in the same way as the concept of number. All this is represented diagramatically in Fig. 3.

Alternatively a form of matrix representation is also useful. Here we must precede each item in the left hand column by the items indicated by 1 in the columns to the right (Fig. 4).

These forms of analysis are not easy but are very necessary. Indeed, the learning of the relationships between topics may be just as importan

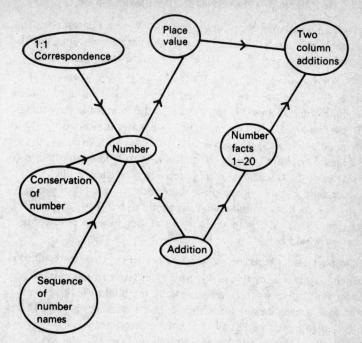

Figure 3

		A	B	C	D	E	F	G	H
Column addition	A		1	1	1	1	1	1	1
Place value	B					1	1	1	1
Number facts 1–20	C				1	1	1	1	1
Addition	D					1	1	1	1
Number	E						1	1	1
Sequence of number names	F								
Conservation of number	G								
1:1 correspondence	H								

Figure 4

or even more so than the topics themselves. We must develop strategies to enable children to learn not only techniques and concepts, but also the relations between them so that the material exists as a whole.

3. *Ordering of material* Fig. 3 left us with a logical hierarchy of topics. This may well not be the best *teaching* order but in planning a teaching order, it should be very much to the fore. An unstructured discovery approach, for example, may well enter the network right in the middle or even at the wrong end! This does not matter so long as the logical relations between the topics are finally re-established. It is a matter of the teacher's knowing precisely what she is doing.

Logically a knowledge of place value and a knowledge of simple number facts *must* precede two-digit addition, but they have no *direct* relation with it. A diagrammatic representation of a direct teaching strategy would be

Simple number facts $\longrightarrow$ place value $\longrightarrow$ two-figure addition

which is again a distortion of the logic. This latter structure is called *linear* for obvious pictorial reasons. Many textbooks use this format in that each topic is completed within its own section or chapter. This is tidy and convenient especially for revision or reference.

There is, however, an alternative strategy. Logically place value occurs before two-figure addition. A child does not, however, become familiar with *all* aspects of place value before proceeding with two-figure addition but only with those involving tens and units. This partial understanding needs to be extended before three-, four- or *n*-figure addition can be undertaken. We thus find ourselves in a situation where the same pattern

place value $\longrightarrow$ addition

repeats itself at ever higher levels of complexity and sophistication. This is known as the *spiral* or *helical* approach to content. It can be a most useful weapon where the emphasis is on teaching a body of material as a whole as opposed to developing a series of individual topics in depth.

4. *Classroom organization* We have already argued in favour of practical work and a consideration of children's individual differences. This implies only limited use for the situation where a class of forty is taught as a single entity. The emphasis needs to be on group or

individual work with progress governed by work cards or similar techniques appropriate to each group's developmental level.

5.   *Motivation*   We are all aware of the child who shows no capacity for school subjects whatsoever, but is a walking encyclopaedia on association football. The difference is one of motivation. He is interested in football but not school. This raises the vital question, how can we motivate children to like mathematics? The attitude of many adults indicates that we have frequently failed in the past. Inefficient rote learning is soon exposed as a result of the precision inherent in mathematics and the result is a mass of wrong examples and the teacher's disapproval. This feedback, for many children, indicates that they cannot possibly do mathematics and they rapidly learn to dislike the subject. If mathematics is treated practically, the children have more chance of understanding, more chance of getting correct results, and more chance of the teacher's approval. Also the practical apparatus itself is often pleasant to handle. Once they have developed a little self-confidence, many people begin to appreciate the very qualities which make mathematics difficult.

6.   *The discovery method*   The essence of the discovery method is that children learn more effectively by making discoveries for themselves than by being directly taught. This apparently simple thesis is difficult to prove or disprove in practice for a variety of reasons.

First of all, discovery methods as usually practised, are, for the very best of reasons, invariably closely linked to practical work. This is right and proper but does not help us to evaluate the relative effectiveness of each aspect.

Secondly, the effectiveness of the method can only be tested against the aims and objectives of the teachers concerned and these, of course, vary from teacher to teacher. The method may be highly successful in developing a positive attitude to mathematics but inadequate for teaching methods of subtraction or any other specific technique.

A third variable is the amount of teacher control over the discovery process. In the extreme case, a child is put into a mathematically stimulating environment to discover what he will. The teacher's role is one of support and encouragement. A more appropriate method for the teaching of specific content would be a carefully controlled situation with chosen problems where children could still make their discoveries but the general nature of these would be known to the teacher who, with expert teaching, would then derive the content skills required. Such methods of guided discovery require great skill on the part of the teacher constructing the situation.

The time element provides yet a fourth problem. Discovery methods are time-consuming compared with other methods from both teacher's and pupil's point of view and a comparison which states that they teach better in more time can hardly be called conclusive.

In some circles discovery mathematics has almost the form of a religious dogma. We prefer to regard it as a satisfying and therefore highly motivating activity. It becomes sound teaching strategy to attempt to capitalize on it, but we must do so with our eyes fully open as to both its strengths and its weaknesses.

7. *Programmed learning and algorithms*   These may be looked upon as providing a complementary approach to discovery methods. Their emphasis is more on content than attitudes and they tend to derive their effect from the pupil's satisfaction at achieving correct results. This approach has made much less impact at primary level than the discovery approach. It has less glamour, smacks of traditional hard grind, and can fall short because of inadequacies in the reading skills of the children concerned. Much, however, can be learnt from the programmer's approach. Programmes in the future should tend to resemble work cards with associated packs of equipment which will be precisely geared to the objectives they seek to realize. They will even contain discovery elements where appropriate.

The algorithm approach is one which can effectively and easily be used by teachers in appropriate circumstances. An algorithm is a precise set of instructions for carrying out a specific task. Originally the word was restricted to a computational process with numbers (e.g. an algorithm for division) but here it is used more generally. Algorithms are usually best presented in the form of a flow diagram. There is a bonus here in that the use of the flow diagrams is a necessary skill in the mathematical repertoire. The use of an algorithm may require relatively little understanding of the material involved. Under certain circumstances, however, it may be argued that the best way of learning how to do something is to actually do it. An example of an algorithm which initially ignores the question of understanding is given in Fig. 5.

To find the area of a leaf or similar shape

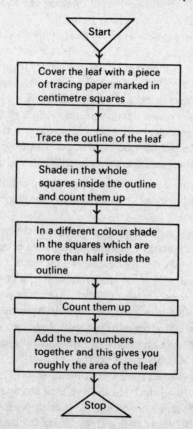

Figure 5

As it stands and out of context this algorithm would enable a child to calculate approximate areas with very little understanding of area. Moreover, the key step for dealing with incomplete squares is given without comment. It is suggested, therefore, that such an algorithm would only be used after the normal concept-developing activities had taken place. It may be argued that the children should discover the above technique rather than be told it, but an alternative strategy is that, having found the area of his leaf, the child has then to explain to his teacher how the technique works. In each case the child has to indulge in some heavy mathematical thinking and should end up by understanding the techniques he is using.

A further more sophisticated use of algorithms occurs when a child discovers a technique of some complexity. He may well be asked to put his technique in the form of a flow diagram for the sake of his teacher and friends. This is indeed a stringent test both of basic understanding and mathematical and literary skills.

In this section we have emphasized the virtues of the algorithmic/ programming approach as being complementary to the discovery approach. This emphasizes the existence of a variety of approaches to mathematic teaching and the need for skilled discrimination in choosing.

8. *Individual differences* We have mentioned child-centred learning with regard to differences both in children's developmental levels and in their motivation.

Another recognized individual difference between children is intelligence as measured by intelligence tests. At primary level in particular this is complicated by developmental levels. Children of the same age can clearly be at different levels of both maturity and intelligence. There are, however, other differences which, although not so immediately obvious as maturity and intelligence, are real enough. We cannot give a full account of the work done on individual differences here but we shall take one example and follow through some of the implications for primary mathematics.

Most readers will be familiar with the introvert/extrovert classification system of C. G. Jung which has been refined and analysed by Professor H. J. Eysenck. Eysenck has turned the dichotomy into a continuous scale which is also linked with a stable/unstable classification so that two extremes would be, for example, a stable introvert and an unstable extrovert.

One of the above extremes is particularly interesting. The traditional classroom situation with its fixed rows of desks and its deathly silence was particularly favourable to the stable introvert, the type of child who was prepared to work for long periods by himself and who did not wish to be involved with other people. Indeed such a child was looked upon with delight by both teachers and parents. Such phrases as 'he's a quiet one' or 'he's a deep one' were indeed expressions of awe and approval. Today, however, the pendulum has swung to the other extreme. Silence is the exception rather than the rule in many primary schools. Group work is favoured at the expense of individual work and the methods are used to 'bring him out' or make him 'join in'. Clearly, all vert at the expense of his sober introvert peers. Indeed the quiet, withdrawn child, previously the pride of our educational system, may now be considered distinctly abnormal and all sorts of unfortunate methods used to 'bring him out' or make him 'join in'. Clearly, all types have a right to exist and to receive an education not fundamentally opposed to their basic nature. Clearly also the stable introvert needs to communicate at least to some extent with society if he is to survive, just as the unstable extrovert needs to get down to individual work. It is extremely doubtful, however, whether attempts to change personality can or should be undertaken within the normal education system, and a system which favours one type of child at the expense of another clearly leaves much to be desired. Now, with the more loosely structured situation of the modern classroom, we have the possibility of a genuinely child-centred education. If a child wishes to work alone, within reasonable limits he should be allowed to do so. If a child always craves company, within reasonable limits he should be allowed to have it. If a child learns more successfully by discovery methods, let him do so. If he finds the algorithmic approach more successful, again good luck to him. This is child-centred learning in the best and most practical use of the term. The difficulties are considerable and so are the implications for the teaching profession and teacher training. It seems to us, however, that this is the only serious possibility for a genuine child-centred approach to the problems of education.

Appendix

Mathematics for life : an essential minimum

If one were to ignore the specific needs of given trades, professions, or academic disciplines and try to determine what mathematics remains in ordinary life, one might arrive at a core of essential mathematical knowledge. One needs to be ruthless in one's pruning, and ask whether the lack of knowledge could be of social or economic consequence to the individual in his daily affairs. It is not our task for this purpose to ask if the knowledge could be interesting or the skill potentially useful, but to ask if lack of it will be a grave disadvantage. The school leaver who lost his first precarious job because he could not fill in his time sheet accurately, is a case in point. He was educationally deprived.

Here is a suggested list of essential topics. No child should leave school without every attempt having been made to cover it. Most children will have more, many children much more, but anyone with less is likely to be a deprived citizen. The list could be of interest to those concerned with backward children.

1. Addition, subtraction, and one digit multiplication for numbers up to two digits.
2. The use of money in daily life—in effect number work to two decimal places, but handled mentally as pounds and pence.
3. All common aspects of time and date, including timetables and the twenty-four-hour clock.
4. Familiarity with the use of (not computation with) the recommended metric units and such imperial measures as continue to be met.
5. Meaning (not computation) of percentages and averages.
6. Understanding very simple statistical graphs as used, for example, by newspapers.
7. Rough estimates of sizes, distances, and costs.
8. Rounding-off measurements.
9. Reading graduated scales.

The above is a minimum and indeed a very bare minimum. It is in no way to be confused with the needs of an educated person as discussed in this chapter. We should regard anyone whose knowledge did not meet this list as likely to run into difficulties at some probably early stage in his career.

References

[1] J. Hadamard, *The psychology of invention in the mathematical field*, Dover, 194

[2] Nuffield Mathematics Project
        Checking up 1,
        Checking up 2, Murray/Chambers, 1970.

Film:

Checking up—children and mathematics, BBC TV Enterprises.

[3] P. H. Hirst and R. S. Peters, *The logic of education*, Routledge and Kegan Paul, 1970.

CHAPTER THREE

THE MATHEMATICAL
AND CONCEPTUAL BACKGROUNDS
OF MATHEMATICS TEACHING AT PRIMARY LEVELS

3.1 Introduction

The history and general character of the elementary arithmetic taught in schools at all levels has often been discussed. In this section we are concerned solely with the implications for the Primary school of what has, rather unfortunately, come to be called 'modern mathematics'. This is merely that part of mathematics developed over the past 150 years or so, which has until recently had little effect on school curricula. We must remind ourselves in passing that the upheaval in school mathematics is only one face of our problem of keeping school curricula in step with our expanding horizons. The new work in mathematics has been easier to assess at secondary levels, and most of the 'modern' topics are now satisfactorily absorbed into recognized examination syllabuses. The influence in the primary school is more indirect and less easy to discuss.

First, we now see from the classroom that mathematics is a developing and expanding subject, and not a once and for all collection of processes, a closed and completed system in which nothing could be discovered or altered. Secondly, there is the modern interest—albeit a revival of an enquiry first conducted by the Greeks—in the nature of mathematics and the logical connection of its parts.

We now think of mathematics in a way caught by Professor W. Sawyer: 'mathematics is the study of all possible patterns'. This, of course, is a comment and not a definition. Our numbers form patterns in tens; and a geometrical diagram is a pattern of lines and points. But today the objects of mathematics extend considerably the simple numbers of ordinary arithmetic or the easily grasped geometrical processes of bisection or construction. It is the implication of this extension that concerns this report. Most of the newer concepts are named and given appropriate treatment in secondary syllabuses: one meets matrices, vectors, transformations; isomorphisms, number systems, finite arithmetics and so on in what is by now a fairly well-defined canon. But what influence should all this have on the primary school?

At this point we must distinguish very firmly between the implications for the teacher and for the children. There are two points:

1. A knowledge of what mathematics will be like at the secondary level is essential for the teacher at primary level.
2. A knowledge of mathematics may reveal unsuspected significance or pattern in work being done at primary level, and may suggest interesting and valuable extensions of that work.

There is, however, no logical step whatever from this position to a decision to introduce the vocabulary and concepts, and still less the symbolism, of newer mathematics into the work of the primary school. Many believe that work in the new topics can be initiated using ordinary language, and that the ideas we wish to convey are only obscured by a barrage of technical terms and symbols. The other point of view is that here is a chance to introduce new words in a meaningful context, to extend the children's vocabularies in action. We hope that this report will achieve a working balance between these two views. We take it that, since very young children can learn difficult words and concepts quite naturally in their home surroundings, there would seem to be a good chance of their acquiring mathematical terms by a similar process.

Different countries have approached these problems in the light of their own traditions and aims, and one can see the results in the different systems advocated by certain American projects or by continental educationalists such as Georges Papy.

Our own primary curriculum in mathematics has always stressed its applications and its function as an aid to describing or understanding the environment. On the Continent, however, primary work is much more subservient to the needs of the secondary stages, so that many long-term developments of mathematical topics are begun at primary levels and can only be completed later. These rely totally on an intrinsic motivation, one which lies within mathematics itself. The continental mathematician and his colleagues in the schools tend to stress the subject as a deductive line of development from certain basic assumptions, and, rightly or wrongly, look for situations to convey the notions regarded as necessary for its logical growth.

A variant on this continental view, commonly found in the United States, is to regard certain ideas as the effective key to much of mathematics, and to convey these ideas as early as possible, even if they can only be clothed in everyday meanings at a later stage in the school course. An interesting example is the American attempt to base the teaching of number and elementary number operations on a prior knowledge of set theory, an attempt which has been applied only in a considerably modified form in this country. We feel that, although it may be true that the number operations can be logically developed from operations with sets, it does not follow that the psychology of the child follows this sophisticated process, any more than the actual history of mathematics followed it.

Against this negative view of the value of key logical concepts, however, there does seem to have emerged from the Nuffield and other experiments a clear idea of practical classification and sorting as a fundamental mathematical *activity*, with the concept of number emerging as a particular mode of classifying sets. Similarly, work with such apparatus as logic blocks, designed to teach the ideas of set algebra and mathematical logic, develops in children familiarity in the precise use of the *vocabulary* of a language. This type of development appears more useful than, say, attempts to explain $2 + 3 = 5$ in terms of the properties of disjoint sets.

In what follows we have tried to collect a few of the key ideas of modern mathematics and to discuss them, both as an integral part of the background of the teacher and as an inspiration for the activities of the class. We have chosen those concepts which can easily be talked about without the technical vocabulary of the specialist: only the names for the concepts can be regarded as peculiar to mathematics, and we hope to show the way in which we recommend knowledge of them to the practitioner in the primary classroom.

3.2   The background to primary mathematics

In many primary schools throughout the country, as evidence that they are trying to do something about modern mathematics, children are asked to produce diagrams like Fig. 6.

In so far as such exercises are suggested and fully described by a number of textbooks currently available, they do not require *necessarily* any particular background on the part of the teacher—only the willingness to abandon exercises in arithmetic in order to find the time to do them.

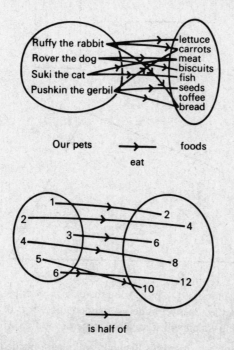

Figure 6

Again, children may be asked to cut a shape from card, a rhombus, say, or something more complicated such as Fig. 7, or even a quadrilateral whose four sides are of different lengths, Fig. 8, and then attempt to make a tessellation with this shape, i.e., to cover a surface without gaps as if it were a tile. This could lead to attempts at generalization. What kinds of shapes form a tessellation, and what have they in common? Can we extend the range of shapes that form a tesselation, by using shapes in pairs?

These activities and many others like them, must be fairly familiar by now and this report will assume that they are. But why do them?

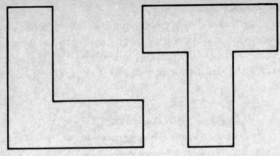

Figure 7

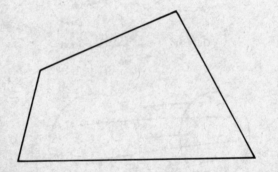

Figure 8

Are they an ingenious attempt to keep the class busy as pleasantly as possible during the times set aside for mathematics, or is there, behind them, something which will serve all or some of the following functions?

1. Connect up with situations the child will meet outside the classroom.
2. Help develop the number skills which society demands all of us should possess.
3. Lead on to more complex concepts at a later stage in education.
4. Link up to form a body of knowledge which, as 'mathematics', has a recognizable existence.
5. Ensure that the less able child has a reasonable chance of making progress without discouragement.
6. Ensure that the really able child is given every opportunity to stretch himself.

7. Fit more easily into any schemes of integrated work or combined study that the school may care to attempt.

Some of these desiderata are clearly educational, but the rest do amount to the question whether or not the traditional courses are being supplanted by something worth doing both for its own sake and as an introduction into a wider field of valuable studies: mathematics itself.

It is precisely at this point that the teacher's own understanding and knowledge becomes important. What does he know of the mathematics of which these activities are the manifestation at primary level?

It should also be clear that a section in a report cannot provide the knowledge that is required. Reduced to the extreme compression of a short handbook, modern mathematics seems either incomprehensible, or, if comprehensible, pointless. But what we can try to do is to extract a few key ideas from these typical activities in the new mathematics, suggest their mathematical importance, and show how they can be discussed with the children without using the language and symbolism of formal modern mathematics.

3.3 Some key concepts in primary mathematics

The remark that 'mathematics studies all possible patterns' is a good starting point for our discussion. It is too vague to generate the subject matter of mathematics, yet anything we actually do in mathematics can be fitted in. A pattern is a scheme, a mould, a reproducible structure, a recognition of a relationship between parts. Mathematics works to abstract such patterns from situations and to give them a formal statement.

The power of mathematics in use lies precisely in this: that its formal statements, abstracted from any physical situations, can be expanded again to enable us to say what will happen in the physical world. Excessive vibration in the wing of an aircraft is analyzed mathematically in much the same way as the rise and fall of the tide at London Bridge; by studying the pattern we can diagnose the one and predict the other.

At the primary stages, then, this suggests that the work should provide a great many situations where the comparison of structure is possible. Most of these situations may be discussed quite informally with children and if not necessary, it is certainly desirable, that the teacher has a more precise idea of what is happening.

Consider, for example, the two diagrams of Fig. 6. They each consist of two sets of entities enclosed in loops and linked by arrows. In one the entities are proper and common nouns, in the other numerals. Is there a mathematically significant difference if we agree to ignore everything except the pattern? Now in the second diagram each member of the one set is connected to each member of the other by a single arrow, and no two of these start or finish at the same point. This is not so in the first diagram. From situations such as these, we derive the key concept of a *one—one correspondence* as shown in the second diagram. Just why this is a key concept is a task for the mathematical educator to make clear, and the responsibility passes to the College of Education, the Teachers' Centre, the in-service course and the private initiative of the individual in his reading.

Now let us develop this concept. The use of coloured rods of the type marketed by Cuisenaire or Color-Factor is both familiar and general. With them, a child learns, by measuring the longer rods against the shorter, to explore relationships between them, and later by choosing a number to be represented by any one of the rods, to set up a one-to-one correspondence between the natural numbers and the rods as identified by their colours. Thus, using an arbitrary colour scheme chosen as an example, we could have, choosing the shortest rod as a unit,

1	White rod
2	Blue rod
:	:
:	:
5	Black rod
:	:
7	Yellow rod

If now we put the rods together end to end, we note that, with an obvious symbolism

$$\text{blue} + \text{black} = \text{yellow}$$

If we consider the corresponding natural numbers we get

$$2 + 5 = 7$$

Here the pattern of the rods put end to end corresponds uniquely to the operation of addition between pairs of numbers. They are, of course, designed for this express purpose. A relation of this kind is called *isomorphism*, and once more we have a key concept recognized throughout mathematics. Its practical importance is fundamental to the art of using mathematics, because we can work with whichever of the systems is convenient. We can either add a set of numbers or we can put a set of rods together and match up their total length. We also do this when we use logarithms: we can either multiply numbers together to get their product, or we can add their logarithms as given in a table, and match up the sum of the logarithms against the required product in the antilogarithm table. The pertinent question is whether teachers who are successfully using colour rods to teach the number facts realize that the underlying principle that makes their apparatus work is also what makes possible the logarithm table and the slide rule.

As a final example, let us take the rod property when lengths are put together:

$$\text{blue} + \text{black} = \text{black} + \text{blue},$$

which is shown diagrammatically in Fig. 9.

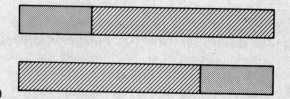

Figure 9

This corresponds to the numerical fact (using the same arbitrary colour-code):

$$2 + 5 = 5 + 2.$$

From examples of this kind, we abstract the so-called *commutative* law which is obeyed by addition and multiplication of numbers. It is important because some processes with some entities do *not* obey it.

For example, with numbers and division $2 \div 3 \neq 3 \div 2$,
and at later stages in mathematics we often meet operations where the issue is by no means obvious.

What is emerging from the foregoing is a series of situations that are described with technical precision in abstract mathematics. We feel that these should be working principles in the teaching of mathematics at all elementary levels, although we would avoid expressing them in the technical language that tends to become jargon out of context. But we ought, nevertheless, to say something positive about these principles. It would then seem part of the teacher's professional skill that he should be able to find the correct form of words.

When the child has successfully grasped $5 + 3 = 8$ as a number fact, known without hesitation as such, should we not ask the question: does it matter if you put the 3 first, or can we do them the other way round? The point here, and it seems to be a crucial one, is that only a person fully aware of the commutative law as such would think of asking this question. Once it is asked, the child begins to learn his number facts in pairs. Having discovered, perhaps from the coloured rods, that 2 lots of 7 are 14, he knows automatically that 7 lots of 2 also make 14

$$7 \times 2 = 2 \times 7$$

and the reputed barrier of the 7-times table is never set up.

This is only one possible pay-off for us from being aware of the abstract rules of arithmetical operations.

Another key pair of concepts is that of *identity* and *inverse*. Here again the two technical terms reflect the recognition in apparently very different mathematical topics of an underlying unity, and once more the underlying unity implies that the disparate topics can be similarly treated.

In any operation such as addition, the *identity* leaves unchanged the original entities. Thus, for ordinary numbers

$$2 + 0 = 2, 3 + 0 = 3, 4 + 0 = 4,$$

and 0 is the *identity with respect to addition*. Similarly 1 is the identity for multiplication. We have here a general concept applied to operations of one mathematical quantity on another, and in secondary and higher mathematics it extends beyond the domain of ordinary numbers.

But mathematics also abstracts from its operations the concept of *inverse*. Any quantity combined with its inverse produces the identity. Thus for multiplication,

$$2 \times \tfrac{1}{2} = 1$$

and $\tfrac{1}{2}$ is the multiplicative inverse of 2;

$$\tfrac{5}{3} \times \tfrac{3}{5} = 1$$

and $\tfrac{3}{5}$ is the multiplicative inverse of $\tfrac{5}{3}$.

We can now formulate questions at class level.

What number multiplied by 2 gives 6?

What number multiplied by 2 gives 1?

and the way is open for the fraction to emerge as an extension of the systems hitherto confined to natural numbers, without any special and *ad hoc* definition.

We recommend strongly that the possibilities of such an approach to the teaching of the multiplication of fractions, taken after experience in the meaning of fractions and perhaps in parallel with more familiar methods, should be carefully considered.

Not only is there a possible implication for classroom methods of these key generalizations in mathematics, but some of its theoretical preoccupations seem full of interest if examples are taken at a suitable level. One of these is the discussion of inductive reasoning. If something turns out to be true for the first, second, third, fourth . . . examples investigated, is it always true?

$$
\begin{aligned}
\text{Consider} \quad 3 + 5 &= 8 \\
17 + 9 &= 26 \\
9 + 21 &= 30
\end{aligned}
$$

Here the addition (odd + odd) produces an even number, and similarly (even + even) produces even. Is this *always* true, or only true because we happen to have chosen suitable numbers? Much technical skill has gone into developing and formulating inductive reasoning in mathematics, but the point here is that we do *see* a pattern. The question, as Wittgenstein asks it, becomes:

Is there in this process, any feature that makes you think you can go on doing it for ever?

The use of Unifix cubes on their grids or a suitable diagram may help to shed light on the situation (Fig. 10).

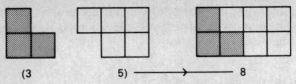

Figure 10

And how do we modify the rule if we multiply, divide or subtract? Surely we have here a fruitful discussion, an unmistakeably intellectual exercise, yet at the level of the primary classroom. One feels that only the confidence that comes from knowledge can lead such a discussion in class; that such a discussion is valuable as a contribution to mental development seems quite certain.

We have now taken examples of key generalizations with one suggestion for mathematical discussion and shown that they can be relevant in the classroom. It will be worth while considering a topic from mathematics—new mathematics only in the sense that it has recently become popular in the new syllabuses—and considering its value at class level.

The numbers

$$2, 5, 8, 11, 14, \ldots,$$

are equivalent (another key term) in the sense that each leaves a remainder of 2 when divided by 3. Since the only possible remainders when numbers are divided by 3 are 0, 1 and 2, it follows that all natural numbers fall into one of three sets or classes, which may be labelled as 0, 1, 2. The discussion of the properties of these three sets, of what, for example, happens if members from the various classes are added or subtracted, forms the topic known as *modular arithmetic*—in this example, *arithmetic modulo 3*. This topic has interest or application outside mathematics, from being a description of what happens with devices such as clocks which count the passing hours to modulo 12 or 24 and with many other forms of meters. It is also important within abstract mathematics in investigating the properties of numbers. It can have a quite useful pay-off as a class topic.

Consider some of these results:

1. Sorting a set of numbers into their classes results in considerable incidental number practice at a level entirely within the capabilities

of any given group of children. Compare the tasks

(a) Separate the numbers from 1–50 into three classes modulo 3
(b) Sort the house numbers of the members of this class into the seven classes modulo 7
(c) Choose numbers at random from a telephone directory and classify them modulo 13.

The wording could, of course, easily avoid technical terms, which are used here for conciseness.

2. If the children operate arithmetically with numbers given their class labels rather than their names, they are restricting themselves to a finite (and usually small) system of numbers.
Thus

$$10 + 11 = 21,$$
$$13 + 14 = 27,$$
$$76 + \ 8 = 84$$

are all reducible to

$$1 + 2 = 0,$$

and we have a system which actually has different rules from those already familiar. In this system, the only numbers are 0, 1, 2 and the addition table becomes the finite pattern

+	0	1	2
0	0	1	2
1	1	2	0
2	2	0	1

3. There is a familiar number practice exercise with such instructions as:

> Using number strips and the number line if necessary
> count in fives starting from 2,
> count in sevens starting from 5.

This process clearly generates successive members of the classes we are considering, so that once more we have a general principle at work behind different activities. The interest and understanding of the teacher might well be stimulated by this.

4. The process links up with a simple geometrical exercise on a clock

face, often described in articles and booklets devoted to primary activities. If we go round a clock face, starting from 12 which is equivalent to zero, (and indeed 'zero hours' is the military and navigational equivalent to 'midnight') to a count of 3, and join up the hour points thus reached by arrow lines (Fig. 11a)

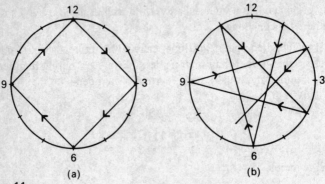

(a)   (b)

Figure 11

we get a square, described clockwise. If we go to a count of 9, we get the same square, described anticlockwise. If we go to a count of 5, beginning from 1 o'clock, we get the pattern shown unfinished in Fig. 11b.

Clearly the investigation of these patterns has considerable scope. We can ask which choices of interval eventually land us up on every hour mark, or what effect choosing a different starting point or dividing the circle into other than 12 parts will have; and the determining factors in the types of pattern obtained are the modular properties of the numbers concerned.

Here again one can obtain the patterns without being fully aware that they are simple illustrations of general abstract theories, but, if only for the teacher's sake, it helps if they can be given a conceptual background.

So far we have recommended an approach which takes the older topics and looks at them in the light of the concepts now taken to be central in the development of mathematics. It is also true that there are new *teaching* approaches which look at some of the traditional topics in a way which is not new mathematically, but is so pedagogically.

Thus the use of a box $\square$ indicating an incomplete statement which becomes complete when a number is inserted, as in

$$2 + \square = 10$$

is only a modified notation for the traditional equation

$$2 + x = 10$$

but because it *is* a different notation, it enables us to make a different approach, cleared of our own preconceptions about official methods of solving equations. If we take it as an incomplete statement, *any* number can be inserted in the box and the instructions can then be:

(a) fill in a number that makes the statement true;
(b) fill in a number that makes the statement false.

The work takes on a linguistic aspect that is wholly lacking from:

solve the equation

$$2 + x = 10.$$

It is also worth noting that if we take

$$2 + \square = 10$$

as a *verbal* statement, with the symbols taking the place of words in an extended construction, then it becomes

true if 'eight' is inserted,
false if 'four' is inserted,
meaningless if 'dog' is inserted.

The notion that truth and falsehood only apply to statements within certain limited ranges of construction is not one to be milled over in the primary school, but adds a certain adult significance to what in traditional courses is dull and repetitive.

We must, however, suggest a certain caution in approach. Not only is much of the actual vocabulary and symbolism of mathematics inappropriate at primary level: it is also inappropriate as a *requirement* (even if it is welcome where it exists) of the primary teacher. We do suggest that the non-specialist student in a College of Education should learn the meaning of one—one correspondence, should be able to use the word isomorphism in context, and should at some time in his career have worked on modular arithmetic. However, we do not suggest that he must, for example, investigate the properties of a set that make it into a vector space, even if we think this should be taken for granted at the levels of the secondary specialists.

The appendix to this report is an attempt to sketch in, with notes at the salient points, the type of professional course which should be provided for the student who proposes to enter primary school. Parts of this should also be made available to the established teacher who wishes to expand his background sufficiently to be able to adopt the 'new' mathematics in his class with a clear understanding.

CHAPTER FOUR

FROM ABACUS TO COMPUTER

Although it is difficult to exaggerate the social and economic importance of the computer revolution, enthusiasts do tend sometimes to
overestimate the case for computer studies in schools. It is, however, the
secondary school that has to face this problem of tempering enthusiasm
with wisdom. The primary teacher merely needs what every educated
man might feel he should have: an appreciation of the nature of the
computer, its powers and its limitations. Computers are being increasingly involved in day to day activities which affect us all and we cannot
afford to be ignorant of these developments. But the computer revolution
is concerned mainly with data processing: it is the ability to store
information rather than to perform abstruse calculation that is modifying
society, and this is not very relevant to the primary school child. There
are, however, some points of contact which will be mentioned later.

Data processing, in fact, is basically simple set theory, but if we take
from the computer its power of storing data and instructions, it finishes
up as a calculating aid. The use of such devices in one form or another is
one of the most noteworthy features of the modern approach to number
work in mathematics.

4.1 The use of calculating devices

Before we discuss specific calculating devices which could be of value
in the primary school their general advantages can be considered.

1. They can stimulate interest in calculating, both because of the
    pleasure gained by mastering their use and operating them and be-
    cause of the interest aroused by the patterns which, not obvious in
    written algorithms, are often more clearly seen when a device such
    as Napier's rods is in use.
2. They can give a better understanding of number structure. Place
    value, or processes such as multiplication (which can be more easily

seen in one of its aspects as repeated addition) are good examples. If the work has already been done they provide valuable reinforcement.

3. They can not only remove the drudgery from long calculation but can enable more realistic examples to be attempted, such as elementary statistical investigations which would normally entail more routine arithmetic than could be managed in class. It is useful not to have to restrict oneself to small and easily handled numbers.

There are two points which require comment. First, the distinction between calculating devices and primary number apparatus is not a firm one. Calculating devices enable children to do arithmetic quickly or conveniently while structural apparatus helps them to grasp number operations and learn number facts. The abacus, for example, can serve both purposes; and the hand calculating machine, which is designed to mechanize arithmetic, works admirably to demonstrate place value or the use of the distributive law in long multiplication. The second and more important point is that calculating devices do not make arithmetical skill obsolete. The use of apparatus generally has suffered from this misconception. Napier's rods and the abacus require a firmer grasp of additive number bonds for their successful operation than ordinary paper-and-pen arithmetic, and their use can develop this knowledge.

The use of mechanical methods raises once more the old question: at what stage in a child's development should he be introduced to written or other methods of calculating and in what order? Attempts to answer this have been largely responsible for much of the rigidly formalized number work in the primary school of yesterday. The best answer is the simplest: that the teacher himself is the one qualified to judge. But the teacher's number symbol may be the child's meaningless squiggle and there seems to be a real need here for research into the difficulties.

4.2   The social demands on the numeracy of the pupil

It is an interesting comment on life both within and outside the classroom that some teachers are still willing to use arithmetical textbooks based on patterns of commercial and technical usage that have long disappeared. The world into which the young child eventually emerges when he leaves school may well be beyond our imagination, but at least we should realize how the business world of today is run.

Consider, for example, vulgar fractions. Our currency and the increasing use of the metric system make a complete familiarity with the use of decimal fractions essential, but call for no skill in calculating with vulgar fractions. Moreover, the engineer and the technician have for years been in the habit of using decimals with imperial units. The quantity surveyor, who before the advent of metrication in building was the only noteworthy professional user of fractions, did in fact handle them with a special arithmetical technique requiring a duodecimal notation. Yet textbooks still devote much space to vulgar fractions at the expense of decimals. We consider that any residual uses of fractions in the future are unlikely to involve denominators other than 3 or powers of 2, and we recommend that such sums as $\frac{3}{7} + \frac{5}{6}$ should be deferred till secondary levels, perhaps until they can be treated generally in the form $\frac{a}{b} + \frac{c}{d}$. It is important to note that a hand calculator which cannot work with vulgar fractions, deals with decimals if, but only if, the user understands them well enough to handle the decimal markers correctly.

It is not the task of the teacher to train his children to be shopkeepers or bank clerks, and we must recognize that anyone adding up long columns of figures or working out endless percentages by hand is already a commercial anachronism. Yet an important fact emerges that, although a simple machine can aid or do routine calculation at a speed that makes school arithmetic inefficient, more and more people need to be numerate and are likely to find themselves using *some* calculation, occasionally against time as in an examination. A knowledge of the principles and processes of arithmetic would seem more and not less essential in the world of the computer. We should surely emphasize the principles of computation rather than spend time unnecessarily in working up speed in performing it.

There is one more numerical skill continually increasing in value. This is the ability to form a rough mental estimate, a skill that has long been necessary for users of the slide rule, but is now becoming of more general value. The decimal notation, for all its simplicity, is always vulnerable to errors in placing the point. If one can see that $2 \cdot 32 \times 3 \cdot 59$ *must* lie between 6 and 12 one really knows more about number and is far less likely to produce nonsense when turning the handle of a calculator, than the person who can only arrive at a value after carefully multiplying 3 digits by 3 digits.

Much of the work in the old primary arithmetic seemed an attempt to show that the British were indeed a race of shopkeepers. But already shops not equipped with automatic tills are becoming rare, and in the large stores that are likely to be the standard shops of the future, one frequently finds button operated change dispensers. We feel that we should learn to live with the supermarket, in the classroom as well as in the High Street.

4.3   The calculating devices available for primary schools

One is tempted to arrange the common devices in some sort of order corresponding to the stages of the child's education. A rough order arises naturally; but the uses of the different devices are so varied, and in some cases so comprehensive, that one would hesitate to try to impose a sequence. The order given here is that of conceptual complexity and we feel that at some time or other during his career the child should handle them all. Most can be used at different levels of sophistication.

1.   *The number track*   This is usually met as the class 100 strip and is thought of as a teaching rather than a calculating device, intended to establish the patterns of tens in addition and subtraction and to show products as the sum of series:

$$na = a + a + a + a + a + a + a + a + \ldots \text{ to } n \text{ terms.}$$

Used in this way with a set of shorter number strips it does, however, become a simple calculator which both provides the answer and teaches the underlying principle. The pupil who knows that $5 + 9 = 14$, by shifting the 9 strip along the track to a count of ten, can *see* that $15 + 9 = 24$, $25 + 9 = 34$, and so on, and there is no need for him to be taught at this stage an algorithm involving carrying and column addition with its attendant verbal rigmarole:

'$5 + 9 = 14$, put down the 4 and carry 1'.

Later of course column addition must be used, but it is not required here and is inefficient in this example.

2. *Addition and multiplication squares* Although quite simple calculations in engineering or science would be impossible without them, one hesitates to call mathematical tables calculating devices. But like the number line, number squares serve the dual purpose of teaching the child, while enabling him to arrive quickly at results. It is sometimes said that the use of these double-entry tables stops a child from learning the number bonds and products, but it would seem at least as likely that their use results in the eventually more effective memorization of the required facts. Any teacher who has taught mathematics at secondary level will know the logarithms of numbers from 2–9 by mere repetition in use. It is suggested that children should make these squares for themselves, recording in them the number bonds from two to twenty at the appropriate stage, and the products less than 100. A stencil can be cut, or a rubber stamp giving a 10 × 10 blank square is easily obtained. The children can then consult them when needed until they are no longer dependent on them. It is quite common to find secondary pupils who do not know these products thoroughly in spite of years of effort by the primary teacher, and for these the product square, carried around as those who needed it carried the 'shopper's table' during the transition to decimal currency, would seem a most effective solution to their difficulties. The memory is sometimes unfrozen by being freed from the stigma of failure, and the products may eventually be memorized.

3. *The abacus* The possibilities of the abacus as a calculating rather than a teaching aid are underestimated in the western world. Its development and use, which (until the spread of literacy in Europe gave a perhaps unfortunate precedence to written methods) is an interesting story. We can see it now in its most developed form in the Japanese *soroban* whose use depends on an unerring knowledge of number bonds learnt in a special form. Given this knowledge, a few minutes practice each day for a week or so enables one to add columns of numbers at an impressive speed. The abacus, however, is not now likely to be accepted as the slide rule has been, and at most one would recommend that the *soroban* or other varieties of abacus should be available in the classroom with an explanatory booklet so that an interested child should be able to investigate possibilities. Its value as a teaching aid will be discussed later. The knowledge that it is used with

remarkable efficiency by adults in the Eastern world should give dignity to its use in school.

4.   *Napier's rods*   Napier's rods or bones were developed in the seventeenth century as a device permitting multiplication without demanding, as our written methods do, an extensive knowledge of the product tables. Their construction is now well known and given in many works on primary mathematics. They are slow in use, and partial products in multiplication by two or more digits have to be written down with each digit in its correct column. Like the abacus, its convenient use depends on a knowledge of the additive number bonds, so that today Napier's rods are best thought of as a teaching aid motivating practice with the bonds. They could be of particular value with older children whose number knowledge is still shaky. One would also feel that a child who could demonstrate the rods in action is unlikely to have any difficulties with multiplication using the ordinary written algorithm.

5.   *Hand calculating machines*   The devices mentioned so far have been mainly of historical interest although they can also serve as useful teaching aids. The hand calculating machine brings the workaday world into the classroom, and provides, incidentally an excellent demonstration of the way arithmetic works. The lever setting machine with full tens transmission best fulfills this secondary role, and for this reason should be the type chosen for school use. The child who has cleared the machine, set 1 on the register, and turned the handle 40 or 50 times is likely to get a new insight into place value. We suggest that as each process is learnt the pupil should have the opportunity of checking it on the machine, and of seeing how quickly long computations may be done. In exploring the machine, children may themselves discover algorithms. The hand machine is expensive, however, and not many primary schools could manage even one per classroom. In the circumstances, it may be deployed most usefully in three ways:

(a)   Occasionally in the classroom to check results and give the child confidence.

(b)   To work realistic examples which would otherwise prove too tedious for pencil and paper calculation.

(c)   To use as a teaching device, along with any other aid that comes to hand, to help the child who is having difficulty or who is ready to advance conceptually.

There are many books on calculating machines and their possible use at various levels; but the teacher needs to work with a machine himself and become fully familiar with it before he can appreciate the possibilities of using it for remedial purposes or for individual investigation. Schools which have in the past hesitated over the expense of investing in a hand calculator which can only work with pure number, will now be helped by the realization that the spread of metrication and the new structure of our currency enables a single machine to cope with all operations in number, currency, or measure. The child's awareness of developments in science or technology can motivate more difficult numerical work. The machine allows him to compute with the large numbers that so often arise if one tries to apply mathematics to practical everyday examples.

4.4   The effect of the computer on the primary school curriculum

We have already pointed out that at the moment the computer has little direct bearing on the primary school. We have also remarked that every educated citizen should, if only in self defence, have an appreciation of its powers. One would feel that the teacher in particular should have this knowledge. It is, however, the peripheral developments around the computer that are likely to be of more interest in the classroom. The use of flow charts, punched cards, and so on have developed as an adjunct to the computer, and the ideas behind these are of value in organizing the breakdown of work into logical steps and easier stages, and in sorting and classifying in a systematic way. Groups of teachers might well meet to discuss situations that lend themselves to systematic organization by flow charts. One hopes that computer appreciation courses will become more and more available to teachers through arrangements made by local authorities. It should be possible for Teachers' Centres to put on lectures, films, and visits to firms or organizations using computers.

CHAPTER FIVE

ACTION ON NUMBER

In general a child's formal primary education does not begin till the age of five and finishes well before adolescence. The word 'primary' is used here in a sense that will not alter if he does in fact transfer to a middle school. Primary education is in part a foundation rather than an end in itself, and this has important consequences in a plan of primary work. One should begin by recognizing:

1. That all children will have had five years' experience of the world before they begin school.
2. Some children will already have begun to make the abstraction that mathematics requires and will use number words easily and fluently, even if some of them lack full understanding.
3. Some children, for whatever reason, will not have had the experiences of the normal child, and some have very low linguistic ability.
4. All children will continue their education beyond the primary stage.

If children continue their education through a middle school the first school will not bear responsibility for transition to the secondary stage, but at the moment there is still, because of secondary demands, a tendency to teach arithmetical processes beyond the pupil's capacity to understand them. One feels that the primary schools should concentrate much more on the truly basic concepts, delaying work aimed at developing manipulative skill until the child is more able to appreciate their relevance.

If we now consider the first three points, it would seem that the progression of the teacher's work in mathematics will consist of three stages. The term 'teacher's work' is used to emphasize that we are not developing a formal syllabus for the child to follow. The stages are:

1. The need to supply some children with the experiences that most children will have had before school begins.
2. The organization of these experiences into the *activity* of the school so that the child begins to develop the appropriate mathematical concepts.

3. The organization of these concepts into a foundation of numerical and spatial understanding.

This last is to be both thought of almost as an end in itself, being knowledge adequate for the child at his own level of development, and as a basis for further and more systematic study later. For the less able child the amount of ground to be covered after this primary course will be quite small, and the organization of his concepts likely to be very gradual. This chapter then is concerned with the work of the primary school in its mathematical aspects and discusses how the work should progress from reception to transfer.

5.1   From pre-school experience through the first two years

It is probably true that most of the work done during the first two years of school, could, for some few children, merely be taking over the experiences of the pre-school stages. If one lists the skills a child should have before he can be considered ready for formal written work in arithmetic one can see that this is so. One can also see what gaps there are for the school to fill in with the rest of the children. The child should:

1. Be able to sort, according to similarities, a collection of miscellaneous objects.
2. Develop, through active participation and discussion, the vocabulary of order—the use, that is, of number in its ordinal aspect and of comparatives that arise in ordering, such as 'larger', 'heavier', and so on. He must distinguish between different uses of the word 'big' and between 'more' in number and 'more' in some other quantity.
3. Be able to recognize collections of objects and patterns in collections implying the concept of a set as an abstract identity.
4. Be able to match sets in one-to-one correspondence.
5. Learn number names and their order in the counting sequences at least up to 10 and preferably up to 20.
6. Be able to match the words in the counting sequence to objects in a one-to-one correspondence.
7. Understand the conservation of cardinal number as applied to a discrete group of permanent objects, recognizing collections as equivalent or distinct if counted.

8. Learn to read and write the number symbols and words, matching them with collections.

This is a formidable list, but the normal child will be more or less at home with most of these except the last, and indeed some children will be able to deal with numerical comparison involving differences, totalling small groups and so on in a practical and informal way. Inadequacy in any of these abilities would be revealed only in discussion with individual children while they are engaged on activities. Some of these activities would merely extend, for the more fortunate child, part of his home experience which his parents might regard as 'something between a hindrance and a help' (Wordsworth, *Michael*, 1. 189). Examples of these activities might include:

Assisting parents in kitchen, garden or garage
Tidying the sewing box
Shopping with mother
Talking about age, height, shoe and clothing sizes
Counting games and nursery rhymes
Board games with dice, building with material such as Lego
Recognizing house, bus and car numbers
Noting significant times such as bedtime
Ordering by age, size, running ability, or authority
Use of a premathematical vocabulary (e.g. all, some, none, many,
    large, small, and other adjectives with degrees of comparison)
Use of fractions half and quarter
Matching by buttoning coats or laying the table
Checking deliveries of milk, stock of eggs, etc.
Playing on the seashore

One of the first tasks of the teacher, then, is to see that the child can work effectively within these experiences and activities, by providing either substitutes or further and more varied activity as appropriate. As long as inadequacies in the kind of experiences listed continue to exist, any formal written work proceeds on an insecure foundation and it would perhaps be better if it did not proceed at all. It is easy to underestimate the skill and insight needed by the infant teacher in assessing the child's initial deficiences. One can note several points over which care is needed:

1. The use of number in quantitative thinking can only occur if the child has mastered the vocabulary of non-quantitative judgements. Although it is not possible to classify a vocabulary rigidly into sections corresponding to the stages in learning, it seems clear that facility in using certain words should come before any attempt to measure or quantify. A typical list of words which children should be able to use freely in conversation before they begin formal mathematics is given as an appendix to this chapter.

2. A knowledge of the number word sequence does not mean that the child can count. Counting is an operation, not a recitation, and the words must be put into exact one-to-one correspondence with objects. Moreover, we point to each object in turn but rest on the last: we do not point to the whole collection.

3. Number skills acquired by children from one district may be lacking in those who live in another. Young children are sent on errands less frequently than a generation ago, but one who lives in an older district with small corner shops is more likely to know about getting change than one who comes from an outlying housing estate whose inhabitants rely on deliveries or weekly visits to a shopping centre.

Apart from the extensive collection of play material in the infant classroom, a set of number boxes or trays seems an effective way to give the child the opportunity to learn the number words and symbols in action. These can be open boxes about the size of shoe boxes, each labelled with one number word and its symbol. The boxes can be filled each day by one or a group of children, sometimes with objects of the same kind, or grouped according to a common property, sometimes with different objects for each number and sometimes with a miscellany in each box. Many number books and commercial wall-charts restrict their illustrations to groups of similar objects (3 kittens, 4 ducks, 5 balls . . .). It is true that we very commonly use numbers with similar or at least related objects, but it is not always so and children often get the impression that numbers can only be used with homogeneous groups. Clearly the use of these boxes should not be continued any longer than necessary. Once a child can fill them properly, there is little point in his continuing this except for his own satisfaction. Instead he could be asked to help record class attendance figures or a similar but more purposeful activity.

Another suggested method for dealing with number in these early stages is to provide the symbols or names written on cards. Given a suitable collection of objects on a table, the child can be asked to count them by placing a card on each object. This emphasizes the matching process which is the essence of counting. Here the match is a multiple one: there is the sound sequence as the numbers are said, the symbol sequence as the cards are put down, and the actual telling off of the objects as they are labelled by the cards.

The purist, who may like to distinguish between the cardinal of the set and the last number in the sequence, could ask the child to prop up the last card against the object last counted: this completes the count and names the cardinal of the collection. It may be helpful for children to use cut-out figures as well, to bring their tactile sense into play.

5.2   Number: notation and operations

A number is, of course, quite distinct from the notation in which it happens to be expressed, and this is in turn distinct from the symbol that represents it. Thus the number of fingers on one hand is 5 in Arabic—Renaissance numerals but V in Roman, while the number of days in a week is 7 in the one and VII in the other. This latter composite symbol represents a different *notation*: the number is not symbolized in its own right but as five plus one plus one. The same number becomes 111 in binary notation, which reduces the symbols to two (0 and 1) and relies in addition on the devices of place-value. It is the choice of a notation that decides the ease and convenience of computation. Our modern algorithms would be almost impossible in Roman numerals. They also depend on a remembered set of number facts: we begin to calculate the product of 976 and 33 by *recalling* the product $6 \times 3 = 18$, and without this knowledge the computation is a non-starter. Napier's Bones, in fact, was a multiplying device for an age that did not know its tables! Hence an early part of the work at primary level is to learn these facts. There is some measure of agreement on the progression of the work, and a scheme such as this would be generally acceptable:

1. Informal number bonding by activities for numbers less than ten.
2. A more systematic treatment of bonds up to 10, with the introduction of the symbols + and −.
3. An extension of the bonds up to 20.
4. The introduction of products and their inverses up to 20.
5. Products and quotients involving numbers up to 100.
6. Notational studies and the processes of arithmetic.

So far we have used the word 'notation' in the sense of a structure for number symbols as in 'binary notation'. It is also used, as in the phrase 'mathematical notation', for the conventions adopted in writing down operations such as addition. At first the child learns to read numbers as *single* symbols, even if, as with 10, 11, . . ., they are fairly soon seen to be composite, and one would defer any work in place value until he is at home with the first five stages listed above. The other kind of notation begins with a recapitulation from stage two, and indeed is the means whereby the treatment is made more systematic.

The informal stage given at the end of the list is very important and should not be hurried. During this stage, which follows the foundation work above the child would:

1. Put together sets of objects and count them, arranging them in patterns.
2. Make drawings of sets of objects, with numerical labelling.
3. Combine, sort, and recombine sets of objects.
4. Make a diagrammatic representation of sets using dots, crosses, or other symbols (i.e. make simple graphs).

During the next stage, although he does not formally study place value, he could well learn to work with bundles or groups of ten, so that he does in fact realize that 12 is 10 + 2. Here again the abstract manipulation of number as a concept succeeds the manipulation of symbols (i.e. the numerals).

The beginning of notational studies proper involves the use of structured apparatus and will be discussed in the next section. By structured apparatus we mean material designed as a model of mathematical systems, and having as its physical structure a counterpart of a mathematical structure. Coloured rods, for example, are intended to model the rational number system. Teachers differ about the value of a historical approach, but the general feeling is that any discussion of the ways the ancients used for recording numbers should only be mentioned after the child has a firm grasp of the modern notation. The entirely misleading account of the *Just So Stories* should be avoided.

The work of items 2–5 would now be seen to imply the recognition of equivalent numerical statements. A triple of numbers gives us the four statements, e.g.

$$(3, 4, 7) \longrightarrow \begin{aligned} 3 + 4 &= 7, \\ 4 + 3 &= 7, \\ 7 - 4 &= 3, \\ 7 - 3 &= 4. \end{aligned}$$

Because of its importance, children should also get used to verbalizing subtraction as complementary addition, for sums up to 20:

$$3 \text{ up to } 7, 4;$$
$$4 \text{ up to } 7, 3.$$

We are in effect introducing subtraction from the very beginning as the inverse of addition. Phrases like 'take away' and 'difference' should be used in appropriate situations only, and not discussed as 'subtraction' until the child himself realizes the parallel. One can also do as above for products and quotients

$$(2, 4, 8) \longrightarrow \begin{aligned} 2 \times 4 &= 8, \\ 4 \times 2 &= 8, \\ 8 \div 2 &= 4, \\ 8 \div 4 &= 2. \end{aligned}$$

Some of the structured apparatus on the market readily demonstrates these equivalences, and makes it possible for the child to learn them together. We do not, of course, suggest that all work in computation should be deferred until these number facts are known completely, because it is clear that work in computation helps impress these facts. The items in the foregoing list overlap one another as they develop, but one feels that the progression should be along the lines indicated.

Our modern number notation and the accepted methods of computation depend entirely on the devices of place value and base. The distinction between these two is seen clearly in the abacus. The base *b* is one more than the number of beads on each wire, the place value is the assignment to each bead of a number b times greater than the number shown by a bead on the preceding wire. The teacher will know that the place values are successive powers of the base, b^n where $n = 0, 1, 2, \ldots$ reading from right to left. For the child the concept is very well introduced by counting with, say, sticks, using singles, bundles, bundles of bundles, where the number in the bundle is the base. It would, of course, be base 10 in most work at this level, although such words as base or power would naturally be avoided. The making up of the bundles of bundles is the key concept, and should come before any attempt to record in writing using place value. At some time during this study children should try to model quite large numbers. If each child in a class of thirty makes forty or so spills from strips of paper put up in in bundles of ten, a four-digit number can be shown with bundles of bundles of bundles (or 10^3). The way in which the pile of material grows is a valuable foundation for the understanding of number.

A useful lead on to the next stage of abstraction could be through the use of short lengths of coloured plastic-covered wire or 'flexi-ties', the wired tape used by gardeners for closing plastic bags. A bundle of five white ties can be bound by a red tie to keep them together. Later the bundle can be represented merely by the red length which now stands for one 5. Similarly a bundle of five reds can be bound with a green tie, which is then 'short for' five 5s, or 5^2. The series can be extended as far as we need.

Many other variations on this theme can be devised, and can be used until the difficult idea of place value begins to be grasped.

In all this early number work the existence of pattern is invaluable in bringing children to an intuitive understanding in which the pattern suggests a general rule or result, although, of course, it does not prove it in any mathematical sense. A study of the 100 square yields many interesting patterns, each of which corresponds to the notational pattern into which the digits fall.

Examples of operation patterns in arithmetic are

$$1 + 11 = 12, \quad 2 + 10 = 12, \quad 3 + 9 = 12, \ldots$$
$$7 + 9 = 16, \quad 7 + 19 = 26, \quad 7 + 29 = 36, \ldots .$$

The last is a useful, and some would say essential, preliminary to systematic notational studies, while a pattern such as

$$3 \div 1 = 3, \qquad 6 \div 2 = 3, \qquad 12 \div 4 = 3, \ldots,$$

prepares the way for later ideas of equivalence. It is one of the marks of good teaching that the seeds of later ideas should continually be sown, so that new topics seem to emerge naturally.

5.3   Structured apparatus and the development of number skills

We have now, at the risk of formalizing what should be informal, discussed early work in number up to the point at which further progress appears to depend on a more systematic treatment. It is at this stage that the structured apparatus, which may well have been already in use informally, begins to play an increasing part in the work of the child. This section is concerned with its use in number work only. Among the many types available, there are several of some importance in any account of this kind.

We shall not attempt a 'best-buy' analysis of this material, although we shall discuss some criteria for assessing it, and we note that some kinds are general apparatus not subject to commercial exploitation, while others are commercially sponsored and subject to design registration or patents.

General apparatus

1.   *Logic blocks*   Opinion is divided on the use of logic blocks. Many feel that sorting boxes containing as much miscellaneous material as the teacher can collect—nails, corks, small pieces of wood, plastic, textiles, and almost anything of a convenient size—provide a more natural starting point than a set of purpose-made articles. Against this it is argued that the blocks give easy control of several variables, with the different attributes of colour, size, and shape readily seen by the children, so that they can be used as the starting point for a penetrating discussion of sorting and classification.

The main purpose of the apparatus is to provide material that demonstrates cross classification and set relations. It does not need any reference to Venn diagrams and the like to put the blocks to use in the early stages of an introduction to sorting.

2. *The number track* This has already been mentioned in the section on calculating devices. As a piece of structured apparatus it has many uses:

(a) It demonstrates the extension of the number series beyond ten.
(b) It establishes, with the help of short number strips, and probably better than any other apparatus, the pattern of tens in addition and subtraction (see p.50).
(c) It establishes multiplication and division as repeated addition and subtraction.
(d) It suggests, later, its own extension as a number *line*. This permits the discussion of fractions and eventually the concept of negative integers and rationals.

There are two ways of constructing a number track which are not equivalent. The first, which really shows number in its cardinal aspect, consists of equal intervals numbered centrally, starting from 1. The second, which shows number as a scalar, numbers the interval divisions and thus starts from 0 like the scale of a ruler.

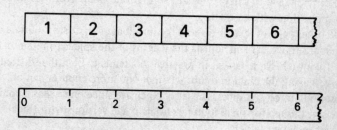

Figure 12   Cardinal and scalar tracks

One would accept that the first form of the track is likely to be most easily handled by young children, but the second has a much more significant structure and it would seem that the effort made to familiarize the child with its use would be well worth while. On this type of track the zero is the point from which one starts to count. The shorter number strips used with a track need to be marked in the same way.

At this stage, recording will have begun and teachers who wish can introduce written addition with two digit numbers

$$15 + 3 = 18,$$
$$14 + 7 = 21.$$

These are done using a supplementary 3-strip or 7-strip. There is no question at this stage of a carrying figure, and nor should sums of this kind be done with counters as this is likely to prolong the period during which the child counts on.

3. *The abacus* As a teaching aid, the abacus in its various forms is useful throughout the whole range of school work, from simple counting to the study of notation. At first the abacus would be merely a bead frame acting as a conveniently anchored set of counters. The existence of the parallel wires or spikes would lead on naturally to the concept of place value, and the use of different colours in the columns gives an added emphasis. Of the bead frame types probably the hoop abacus is the best design, since it keeps the unused beads out of sight behind the partition. By making the hoop frame tall enough the first wire can be made to carry 19 beads, so that one can perform column decomposition with base ten.

Another type of abacus offered for multibase work uses counters of a standard thickness and adjusts the lengths of the spikes to retain only $n - 1$ counters for a base n. In practice this tends to be rather difficult to use, leaving the child in doubt whether one more counter can or cannot be put on the spike. It is also expensive since one needs a complete set, though for small numbers home-made versions with thick washers may be useful.

The work on the abacus can parallel some of the work on the number track. To repeat

$$14 + 7 = 21$$

on a two wire hoop abacus with 19 beads on the first wire helps to make it clear what the carrying figure is actually doing. It can appear as in Fig. 13.

Using a 9-bead abacus, the same addition would appear as shown in Fig. 14, and the transition is made.

The later use of the abacus as a calculating device, preferably in the form of the 5/10 split-base *soroban*, is only possible after the

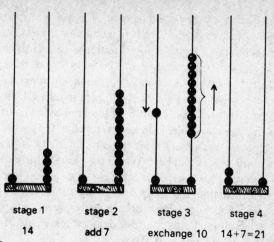

stage 1   stage 2   stage 3   stage 4

14   add 7   exchange 10   14+7=21

Figure 13

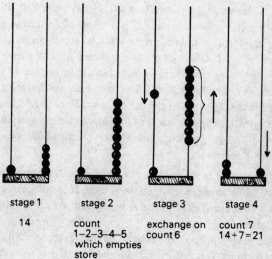

stage 1   stage 2   stage 3   stage 4

14   count 1–2–3–4–5 which empties store   exchange on count 6   count 7 14+7=21

Figure 14

positional notation is fully known—this use helps to develop number skills and might prove interesting for some few children.

4.   *The equalizer or mathematical balance*   This piece of apparatus must be look at with caution. It tends to be unreliable mechanically and has a rather dubious logical status. Friction at the pivot, bending of the hooks and cumulative slight errors in the masses of the washers make it essential to keep a check on its operation, ensuring that it is balancing properly within the limits of accuracy required. Its use does, of course, imply that the child is aware of the implications of balance and imbalance. The main objection, however, is that it uses the principle of moments to demonstrate the commutativity of products and the distribution of multiplication over addition. In the pupil's later science lessons, it is likely that he is going to use an almost identical apparatus to demonstrate the principle of moments using the known properties of multiplication! There does, however, seem to be no objection to the informal use of the device as a 'backing up' piece providing a general experience of balancing.

We give no detailed comments on commercial material such as Cuisenaire, Color-Factor, Stern, Dienes, Unifix, and so on, all of which is supplied with explanatory literature. We merely note that the teacher is faced with a clamorous assembly of purveyors of apparatus designed to help the child learn number facts in schools. Many teachers, examining what is offered, find it hard to form a clear idea of which material is likely to meet their own requirements. No doubt one could try to assemble their opinions and decide on a 'best buy' system for any age group, but for the purposes of this report we shall merely discuss the principle on which any assessment can be based. One can begin by listing some of the dangers that arise when apparatus is in use, and some general observations.

1.   Traditional arithmetic must not be carried on as an independent activity while structured apparatus is used. It is not unknown for a class to do 'arithmetic' in the morning and work with apparatus in the afternoon.

2.   Structured apparatus is intended to be used systematically over a period of years. It is not intended to be dropped as soon as the child can cope with his first written arithmetic, but to be returned to again and again as circumstances require it.

3.   Number apparatus is not intended to be reserved for the backward,

or to be used merely as a prop for the child while he learns written computation. It is meant to give an insight at all levels of primary learning that is scarcely possible without it, and its use may well extend to more advanced levels.

4. A given set of apparatus should not be seen as the sole activity of use to a child apart from work with pencil and paper. Everyday material should be used in parallel with it, so that it is part of an ever-widening number experience and not a restriction on it.

5. Where structured apparatus is in use in an infant school, this fact should be known and appreciated in the junior school into which the child is transferred, and similarly at the next stage. Any apparatus used at one level of teaching should match that used at earlier or later levels. Where possible a phased transition from one kind of material to another compatible with it should be made, e.g., from coloured rods to multibase blocks, without necessarily completely abandoning the former.

6. Teachers will naturally wish to be aware of both the potential and the limitations of the material they have offered to them, and will accept that some experience of its use is needed before the full potential can be realized. To make a child work through the book provided can hardly satisfy the experienced teacher who would often feel that any textbook would need to be adapted to suit any particular child.

The assessment of structured apparatus

Structured apparatus tends to suffer from its origins. Most of it has been developed by enthusiastic innovators and eventually taken over as a commercial proposition. It is sometimes offered by its sponsors as all things to all children: a complete course in mathematics packed in a box. One feels that the most sensible way to deal with it is to discount the claims made by the suppliers and to assess it from scratch in the light of whatever requirements we wish it to meet in the classroom. Any apparatus that has survived commercially presumably does so because it works in the classroom, but it is clear that not all aspects of number or number operations are modelled equally well by all types of material. We shall list some questions that the teacher needs to ask. One would suggest a rough three-point scale for assessment: a particular apparatus will meet a requirement outstandingly well, adequately, or less adequately than one would wish. Local teacher groups may care to devote a few useful meetings to the discussion.

Here then are questions concerning the mathematical structures of the apparatus:

1. What is the fundamental approach to number made by the apparatus? Does it see a number primarily as assigned to an assembly of units or counters, however modified by the actual apparatus, or does it see number basically as a ratio, as a comparison between measures?

2. Does it clearly illustrate number in its cardinal aspect, as the number of a set of objects or units?

3. Does it illustrate ordinal number, the arrangement in a sequence according to some criterion which can be put into correspondence with the number series?

4. Does it demonstrate the concept of place value in such a way that the child moves easily from the use of the material to the recording of what he has done in positional notation?

5. Does it make equally clear the four operations of addition, subtraction, multiplication, and division? In particular, does it show multiplication only as continued addition, or in any other way. Do subtraction and division appear as inverse processes?

6. Does it lend itself to working with subtraction and division in all their aspects?

7. Do the formal laws of arithmetic arise naturally from the use of the apparatus, so that without having to discuss them as such, it can immediately be seen whether an operation is commutative, associative, or distributive over another?

There are also some questions which relate to the use of the material in the classroom, quite apart from its mathematical value, and here the teacher's own subjective judgement comes into play. Such questions are these:

8. Is the apparatus immediately checkable in use? Can the teacher see at a glance whether or not the child is arriving at the required result or does he have to count up pieces for himself?

9. Is the apparatus of a size suitable to the manipulative skills of the age group for which it is intended?

10. Does the operation of the material depend on dimensional stability, with parts which fit or match together? If so can the parts warp or wear even in normal use? Can the material stand up to the sort of misuse one might reasonably expect?

11. What use is made of colour? Is it used

   (a) to brighten up the material without specific function?
   (b) to help identify pieces readily?
   (c) structurally to display number facts?

   If (c) is true, does the use of the apparatus depend on the colour, and is this unambiguously successful?

12. Can the apparatus easily lead to erroneous or misleading results through accidental misuse, e.g., by dropping or miscounting pieces?

13. Does the apparatus depend on a dimensional module, and if so is this metric? This will make no difference to the purely logical structure but could be important if any subsidiary uses are possible, or if the material is used with square paper.

14. Do the elements of the set lend themselves usefully to activities in the classroom which are not primarily intended as 'mathematics' and as bridges for ideas?

Some apparatus is available which goes beyond primary number work and is, for example, more suited to the introduction of algebraic concepts at the top of the school. One must first be quite sure that the children are at such a stage that one wishes to operate in this area. There is much to be said for leaving any systematic introduction to algebra till the 12+ stage, where it can be presented in its more modern forms, but there may be a place for informal approaches earlier. The more sophisticated algebraical apparatus is, however, likely to be of interest to the teacher himself, operating as it does at a level which illuminates his own concepts.

Appendix

An initial vocabulary for mathematics

This list must be considered with caution.

We think that these words, or a list of similar words, should in fact be deliberately checked by the infant teacher, but not, of course, in any formal way. They should be used in a context of ordinary speech with comparatives and superlatives where relevant. If a child is at all hazy about their use, he is not ready for much in the way of school work and he is certainly not ready for number studies.

Obviously, one does not call for definitions, but one uses the words operationally. If, for example, one has handy a few plastic shapes of various kinds, one can say to the child: 'Bring me the square tile (or shape)'. If he cannot select this one immediately, then something is lacking, and he is not ready to embark on any formal or semi-formal work on shapes. Moreover, the words would be used over a long period: they are not a form of reading-age test. If a teacher should feel that any words are included unnecessarily, she should delete them, and she can add any others whose omission she regrets. The list is more an example than a proposed schedule.

The words are given a rough classification for convenience. Our only plea is that all children should be quite familiar with such words as these in context; and the reception teacher knows how often this familiarity may be lacking. If immigrant children are concerned, this operational recognition of words becomes doubly important. Some words like 'full' or 'level' have a fairly precise meaning, but many depend on context. A lot of sugar in a cup of tea is not the same as a lot of sugar in a bowl, and a steep hill is less steep than a steep roof.

Concepts allowing ordering or quantitative judgement

big	same	double	less	small	light
different	enough	lot	more	great	empty
few	amount	twice	weight	several	huge
tiny	full	heavy	large	many	heavy

Spatial concepts: shape and measure

long	line	fat	high	piece	edge
across	square	straight	corner	low	round
point	tall	thin	deep	thick	narrow
size	short	wide	width	shallow	level
quarter	shape	circle	length	half	pointed
blunt	sharp	slope	steep	part	bend
separate	broad	hollow	solid	flat	curved

Time and movement

time	turn	night	quick	speed	year
week	roll	tomorrow	minute	yesterday	late
early	day	slow	morning	still	age
today	month	o'clock	afternoon	fast	move

Money and shopping

buy	sell	save	spend	note	coin
price	worth	change	cost	earn	stamp

(With the recognition and naming of coins)

Position and positional relationships

in	up	out	down	over	under
after	left	right	last	next	near
start	finish	side	front	bottom	before
inside	middle	outside	under	behind	backward
between	sideways	beside	forward	beginning	touch
end	top	far	above	close	back

Logical terms

each	all	some	none	nothing	only
right	wrong	true	include	except	every

Cardinal and ordinal number words up to ten (or beyond, up to twenty).

CHAPTER SIX

NUMBER IN ACTION

The previous section outlined an approach to the teaching of basic number skills, of certain simple properties of the natural numbers, and the operations by which they can be combined and manipulated. In so far as the process of counting and recording is actually number in action, the work already discussed is immediately applicable to situations that arise within or outside the classroom. These are, however, of a rather simple nature. Once number is put into action in more sophisticated ways, the natural numbers cease to be adequate for all purposes.

A situation of everyday importance where this happens is in *measurements*—something we do in practice nearly as often as we make a simple count. At first, indeed, the child does measure by counting: he puts his rule, which is a rod of units, beside the object to be measured, and counts. Later he reads off the count from the numbered units marked on it, and, usually, ignores any discrepancy. Later, if pressed, he may report a length as 'ten and a bit' or 'a bit bigger than ten', but this can easily be found inadequate if something is being cut to fit. It is from an attempt to quantify 'bits of', or the parallel situation of wanting to divide something into parts, that the need for the fraction arises.

Since counting and measurement, with the operations in number that arise from them, will form the bulk of the applicable number work done at primary level—particularly if 'cost' is regarded as a measure of monetary value and 'weight' as a measure of mass—then the skills in measurement and the extensions to the number system required by them are to be considered as essential primary topics.

This is not to suggest that there is only one road to be followed, beginning from simple measurement and leading to all the operations with fractions. We have already recommended (Chapter 3) the possibility of an approach to the teaching of operations with fractions using the concept of an inverse multiplier, and the key concept of equivalence will be likewise invaluable. But the fraction does not intuitively originate in this way: it is from activities such as sub-dividing that the concept is grasped and it is then applied in measuring.

We suggest then, that the work done in measuring and computing in measures should at all stages move in step with work done in extending and understanding the number system beyond operations with the natural numbers.

We must also recognize that the words half, quarter, and third (at least) are essentially premathematical, preceding mathematical notation and being indeed older than the art of writing: what arithmetic has done is to record these words using the numeral signs and then to generalize the concept in the form a/b, where a and b can be any whole numbers, except that b cannot be zero. It is, of course, provisos of this kind, and the possible queries that may arise if a is zero, that underline the need for mathematical understanding on the part of the teacher.

6.1 Measure

The art of measuring is a technical skill not part of mathematics as such, but because measures are expressed numerically and manipulated by arithmetical processes, measure is usually dealt with by the mathematics teacher. In the primary school, measure must be thought of as one of the many concepts that the child must learn to handle. It gives rise to number work in a meaningful context, and hence we welcome it in planning our courses.

The ability to measure grows out of general experience, conversation, and play rather than from special lessons geared to the teaching of its specific concepts. One does not start measure by planning a lesson on 'length'. Before any kind of measurement can begin, the child must understand what it is he is trying to measure, and we refer the reader to Chapter 1 for relevant comments. The child who puts a ruler alongside an object as instructed does not necessarily grasp the concept of length, and many a child who has learnt to say 'area is length times breadth' has a very imperfect idea of what is meant by a surface.

He must, moreover, for this purpose, use a vocabulary in a standard way. If he says 'I am bigger than you', does he always mean 'taller than'? The point arises because it is not certain in what order measures of dimensions should be taken. Euclid puts them in the order length, area, volume; and this has been the tradition ever since. But we live in a world of three dimensions, and it is from this world that we get our first ideas of comparative size and the stabilities of dimension that we now, since the work of Piaget, label 'ideas of conservation'. It is probable that a child actually grasps conservation of volume before that of length, and indeed things change length by stretching and shrinking more obviously than they swell or diminish in bulk. Note, however, how a fish tank of water diminishes by evaporation!

For all that, we feel that since length, area, volume are all three abstracted from the concept of extension in space, and that since this abstraction is most easily done with length, here is a convenient starting point for quantitative treatment of measure. Moreover, children need to begin where the quantities are at first capable of direct comparison, where the inequality or equality of the quantity can be seen intuitively before any attempt is made to quantify it. This is more easily seen with length, although even here the obvious distinction between a straight rod and a tangled skein of wool obscures the issue when one asks which is the longer.

It should also be noted that, between the first recognition that one stick is longer than another and the attempt to quantify the difference by measurement, comes the concept of ordering by magnitudes. Such ordering does not, at first, require measuring instruments, although it is later instructive to order with their aid when one's senses prove inadequate. Thus a child can easily order grossly different masses, say of clay, in wholly irregular shapes by balancing them in his hand, but he will come later to use a weighing device in cases for which the differences are otherwise undetectable.

There has been much writing and discussion about the nature of measurement, and the conditions that must be met before we can have a valid measure. Whether it is or is not possible to give a measure to intelligence as we give one to capacity is still a live topic of controversy; but, fortunately, at the primary level, the logical needs that must be satisfied before something can be said to be measured are, for the most part, met by the simple physical quantities we handle.

One of the simplest of these, which suggests that children should handle the relevant measures long before they pass over to more subtle considerations, is that the quantities should be *additive*. Two lengths, put together, make a greater length whose measure is the sum of the original measures. This *isomorphism* with numbers in addition has already been mentioned in Chapter 3 and it is fundamental to computations with measure. Its importance is not fully grasped until one is familiar with measures which are *not* additive. Temperature is the example most likely to arise at primary level, and detailed discussion should thus be deferred until additive measures have been fully treated.

The teacher should also be aware—although the child need not—of the distinction between fundamental and derived units. Thus the unit of length is, in our system, a fundamental unit, a physical (and legal) standard we can reproduce and use for comparison—the standard international metre. Area, however, is *derived*, and depends on the metre. Its unit is the amount of surface enclosed by the edges of a metre square. So, similarly, speed and density are derived units.

One may remark, however, that the use of the word 'fundamental' here can be misleading. The measures are not logically or physically fundamental, they are merely taken as such for the convenience of the system. Astronomers frequently find it convenient to take speed as fundamental, with the velocity of light as the unit. In this system length or distance becomes a derived unit, the light-year defined as the distance light travels in one year. There are many other examples. The fundamental units that will appear in primary work are now listed. They are:—

Length	—the metre, its multiples and submultiples
Mass	—the kilogram, its multiples and submultiples
Time	—the second, its multiples and submultiples
Temperature	—the degree Celsius (formerly the degree Centigrade in England)
Angle	—the degree

All other measures of area, volume, or speed are derived from these.

Imperial, Metric and SI units At this stage a comment is needed on Imperial measure, on the metric system and the SI or Système Internationale (des Poids et Mesures), better anglicized as Standard International. The SI system merely adapts existing metric and other measures into a consistent form suitable for science, technology and (of considerable importance) international legal contracts. In so doing it has standardized the notation, and we can only repeat that schools should, as textbooks and examination syllabuses indeed are already doing, adopt this notation without delay. The metric system, in the form described in older textbooks and taught a generation ago in the schools, has been absorbed into SI and is of historic interest only— although for practical purposes its units are the core of the system, and some of its units will remain in everyday use. Of the Imperial system— except to note the superb irrelevance of its name—the most that need be said is that its units have, over the centuries, entered into our speech and are likely to remain there as a picturesque reminder of a pre-industrial era. We shall doubtless continue to say: 'Give him an inch and he'll take an ell'. We shall also go on using these measures in daily life for some time, but this does not mean that children must learn to *compute* with them.

We must, however, realize that the SI units were devised for adult use in the worlds of science, technology, and commerce. They are not necessarily suitable for adoption without change in the early stages of education. Unfortunately, there is a misapprehension that schools have been recommended to adopt SI measures in the form laid down, and to avoid the use of the centimetre and the decimetre. This is nonsense.

Perhaps we may quote from a letter written to *The Guardian* in August 1970, by the Director of the Metrication Board:

> 'It is not true that the millimetre will be the basic everyday unit: we shall use the range of units to meet differing needs. For most ordinary purposes such as measuring the width of cloth, the sizes of clothing, and our own vital statistics, the centimetre will be used . . . Going metric will not deprive us of fractions where they are convenient: we can continue to count in halves and quarters as well as in twos, tens and dozens. We shall need to bother no more than we do now with logarithms. Our children are benefitting already in school from the simplicity of metric measures.'

The recommendations have been so widely distributed that they must by now be familiar, but we add (in Appendix 1 on p.90), as a help to living with the metric measures, a list of reference objects whose approximate measurements can gradually become familiar.

Appendix 2 on p.91 gives a complete statement of the SI measures as they will be needed at primary level.

Length

We can now suggest, with comments, the development of a topic in measure, taking length as an example, in order to extend the treatment of Chapter 1.

1. *The prequantitative experiences* The use in context of words like big, small, long, short, their comparatives and superlatives; ordering by eye or by direct comparison of objects.

2. *Towards the quantitative* The use of an arbitrary standard with common objects such as sticks, pencils, etc. (Tradition, based on the history of measure, suggests spans, cubits, paces and so on, whose deficiencies as *standards* become manifest in use. There is, however, apart from the practical difficulties, a case for introducing the standard before these, and only later making comparison between its convenience and the erratic nature of earlier attempts to construct units. The use of the standard should not be delayed once the need for it is realized).

3. *The introduction of the standard* We recommend strongly the undivided metre rod, used along corridors, in playgrounds, or across classrooms. The technique of using just one rod, of measuring along a line and marking the end points (two rods are useful here) must become thoroughly familiar. Chapter 1 is again relevant.

4. *Subdivision of the standard* We suggest separate rods
   (a) metres marked in halves ($\frac{1}{2}$ m divisions)
   (b) metres marked in quarters ($\frac{1}{4}$ m divisions)
   (c) metres marked in tenths ($\frac{1}{10}$ m divisions)

   Note the use of the phrase half a metre and the symbols $\frac{1}{2}$ m, $\frac{1}{4}$ m. These will be needed, will be used and are already used on the Continent. The third rod divided into tenths is important, and will help to bridge the conceptual gap between the notation for vulgar decimal fractions, although at this stage, we would not introduce the word decimetre.

5. *Multiples and submultiples of the metre in the SI system, with the decimal notation* We suggest this order:

(a) Introduction of the centimetre as one hundredth of a metre, but measuring and recording in whole centimetres (e.g. 223 cm not 2·23 m)

(b) Recording in metres and tenths using the decimal notation (e.g. 2·3 m). The word decimetre can be mentioned. Its only technical use as a unit is in marking the draught of ships, but, by giving a name to 0·1 m, it could well prove of value in teaching. Deci- is moreover, a useful prefix met in other words (decimal, decimate, etc.)

(c) The use of the kilometre, whole kilometres, and half-kilometres. For shorter distances use metres. One would consider distances from home to school, or the ground covered during a walk. There is, for older children, the link-up with international athletics, although here metres tend to be used rather than kilometres.

(d) The use of the millimetre in recording smaller intervals with precision. The millimetre is used as the unit (e.g. 23 mm not 2·3 cm or 0·23m). It would only be used by older children.

We must here make quite specific recommendations about the use of the decimal notation in measurement.

The decimetre and the centimetre, giving substance to 0·1 and 0·01 by attaching them to the metre, can well be valuable aids to teaching the decimal notation, but we must stress that measurement is a technique required by society and is only an incidental bonus as a teaching aid. The SI recommendation for submultiples of the units are intended to avoid decimal points where possible. All detailed dimensions in technical drawing should be in millimetres and all drug doses in milligrams or millilitres, so that there can be no doubt where the decimal point ought to be. The decimal point is not used *where it can conveniently be avoided.*

It is equally true that need for recording to 1 or 2 places of decimals cannot conveniently be removed altogether. We shall frequently meet 2·7 km or 1·36 kg and children must become familiar with this notation. But there is not in general justification for writing 12·3 cm rather than 123 mm or 0·78 m rather than 78 cm. Further discussion on this matter is more appropriate perhaps at secondary levels, but it would seem that the SI recommendations for small sub-units are both practically and theoretically sound, and should be acted on in class as far as possible. Common sense is a better guide than a set of rules.

Mass

What has been said about length applies to mass with certain reservations which arise because

1. the range of measurement is commonly much smaller, at least in the primary classroom;
2. apparatus for balancing and weighing is more varied and complicated.

As the kilogram is too heavy for small children, it seems sensible to develop the concept of weight without standard units in the first two years. One then introduces them at Junior level. One can begin with the kilogram and its fractional parts $\frac{1}{2}$ kg and $\frac{1}{4}$ kg. It would probably be advisable to paste labels over the 500 g and 250 g markings which are likely to be found on the weights commercially available. These can be compared with ordinary weights once the gram is introduced. One would suggest that the gram should be named and possibly handled, but that it should not actually be used, at least until the children are quite familiar with weighing. The first work can be done with

200 g, 100 g, 50 g, and perhaps 20 g.

An ordinary pair of classroom scales of the pan type is not sensitive to much less than 10 g anyway.

The work leads to recording in kilograms and fractions, in grams to the nearest 50 g, and later to 10 g. Later still one works in kilograms to one or two decimal places. Recording in kilograms to three decimal places (e.g. 2·165 kg) will *not* arise since no classroom or domestic balance has four-figure accuracy. Some teachers will feel that an interim use of the officially proscribed mixed units, as in 1 kg 250 g, is a useful stage in learning to handle the decimal notation, but this will depend on the teacher. Most teachers are very doubtful of the value of this, and feel that the decimal point can be used as soon as needed.

Mathematically, there is an interesting distinction between the pan balance and the spring or lever balance which is calibrated for direct reading. The balance weighs in discrete increments, the other for all practical purposes gives a continuous reading. The classroom result of this is, of course, the implied need for *interpolation*. One feels, however, that the matter should be raised only with caution. Using a 1 kg by 10 g dial balance, one would say 'it is nearer 120 than 130 and so we'll call it 120 g.'

There are two additional comments which arise in discussing work in the classroom. The first is that, although weighing by balancing against the actual unit and its submultiples is of the utmost importance in teaching, the apparatus that uses this principle is becoming obsolete. One can see scales and sets of weights in use in shops and factories, but one has to look for them, and one finds that they have been almost completely supplanted by weighing machines with a direct reading dial. The spring type, again with a dial, is the only one commonly obtainable in hardware stores for domestic use.

The other is about the distinction between mass and weight. The distinction made in science and modern technology is perfectly clear and unambiguous, but it is not clear either in everyday speech or even in the more sophisticated usages of literary English. Consistent use of SI units at secondary level will solve the problem for the teacher of physics or applied mathematics, but for primary work we propose to cut the knot by suggesting that no great fuss should be made about the distinction. The word 'weight' should be used according to common custom, although we feel that the teacher can use the word 'mass' where he knows it to be more appropriate, so that the children at least meet the word in correct context.

It is true that the child today is much more likely to be aware of a distinction between weight and mass since the weightlessness of an orbiting astronaut is a matter of common information or even understanding. So, too, the teacher himself might be aware of the logical difference between inertial mass and gravitational mass, but this will not directly affect the work of the class.

Computation with mass and length

Traditionally, the teaching of measure has been accompanied by application of the Four Rules to each of the measures as it is introduced. This has been done both by direct use of numerical examples and by verbal 'problems', for the most part given a commercial or simple technical slant to have the appearance of arithmetic in action. So much fun has been poked at the stock examples that it cannot be of value to note them here. It would be an interesting project for a Teachers' Centre to find out just what calculations are done by trades and professions practised in the area served by a given group of schools, and to combine with these any necessary domestic computations that have actually arisen. This surely, would be a good start for a scheme of computational arithmetic. If we remove from the list those calculations that are restricted to a particular trade, and hence appropriate if at all to the secondary pupil, or ignore those which concern the householder a few times only during his adult life, like the tasks of mortgages or wall-to-wall carpeting, which are again not of primary interest, then what are left become the basis and essentials of our work scheme. If this cuts down the standard computations of an earlier generation to a remarkable degree, then indeed it leaves time for newer, more leisurely, and more thorough approaches to number work. It also cuts down the time spent on working with measures, and we must ensure that children continue to get sufficiently varied experiences to enable them to form the concepts on which measure depends.

So far, for our work with measures, we are likely to have a need for the following number skills apart from integer operations:

1. Addition and subtraction of vulgar fractions with denominators 2 and 4.
2. Addition and subtraction of decimals to 2 places.
3. Multiplication of fractions, including decimals by integers.
4. Division by small integers.

As a comment on skill 3, one would point out that many articles purchased by housewives in their daily shopping cost less than 25p, and those purchased by children much less. Indeed the average supermarket checkout bill is less than £1. Hence the young calculator, whatever he does in class, is unlikely to meet in real life items other than, for example

> 3 packets sugar @ $8\frac{1}{2}$p per packet
> $4\frac{1}{2}$ metres (or yards) of flex at 12p per metre.

That more should be attempted, up to limits set by the teacher's own judgement or the child's own interests, is only to be expected; but it is calculation at the level suggested above that is essential. Great care must be taken to avoid artificial problems.

Area and volume

These are derived units and are, in fact as well as in logic, more complicated to deal with. It is their link with *shape* that must be made clear and essential premeasurement activity would consist in a great deal of work with patterns, cutting up and reassembling laminae and building up solids from a given number of bricks so that the concept of conservation emerges. To compare and to put in order without measurement, straightforward enough with length and mass, now becomes difficult unless there are gross differences, or the areas and volumes to be compared have similar shapes or are such that one may be included in the other. There is also the obvious difference between solids and liquids, which has resulted in the distinct terms volume and capacity, whose equivalence is far from obvious; indeed in terms of accepted usage, it may not hold. Is the volume of a sponge the same as its capacity? There is also the difference between space occupied and 'space' displaced. What is the volume of a dandelion seed head? We clearly have a complicated set of concepts.

A query on the comparison of irregular areas suggests the use both of tessellation units and squared paper, with experiment and discussion leading to the choice of a square as a unit. A link-up with length suggests the metre square and the centimetre square as suitable for common ranges of surfaces.

Since the child's early experience of liquid capacity is not only pre-school but is pre-speech, the unit of capacity can be developed from cupfuls and bucketfuls and does not need to wait till the work with the square can be extended to three dimensions to suggest the decimetre cube and the centimetre cube as units. It follows that the litre measure in various forms can be part of the equipment of the reception class. (Plastic squash bottles marked 35 fl. oz. in fact hold one litre, and can be labelled as such).

The work in area, volume and capacity might then present itself in a parallel development such as this:

Capacity and volume	*Area*
Early experiences of toy boxes, playhouses, cupfuls, spoonfuls.	Early experiences of surfaces in crawling, and playing on floors and lawns, feeling up doors to reach handles.

Capacity and volume

Informal activities with water, sand, clay, bricks, and appropriate language.

Conservation situations.

Relations of container dimensions (weight, cross section, etc.).

Comparison of quantities with water, clay, sand , blocks, etc.

Ordering of blocks, vessels, lumps, etc. by size.

Arbitrary standards of measure, with recording by charts and graphs, and the idea of graduating a measure.

Introduction of standard units.

Capacity of buckets and cans in litres, with graduation.

Half and quarter litres.

The capacity–volume relation $(1\ell = 1 \text{ dm}^3 = 1000 \text{ cm}^3)$.

Area

Use of surfaces for drawing, writing, playing. Wiping of tables.

Toy farms and villages on baseboards.

Tessellations with play tiles or blocks.

Conservation situations.

Dissection and reassembly games (Tangrams, jigsaws).

Nests of cuboids.

Shapes which do or do not fit together.

Repeating patterns and tessellations.

Arbitrary units of area.

Measure of actual areas in arbitrary units.

Transition to square units (via tessellation).

Introduction of standard units.

Areas of irregular shapes in standard units (cm^2).

Techniques for counting the square units.

Calculation of areas for rectangular shapes using appropriate units.

Capacity and volume   *Area*

The capacity   volume relation
$(1 \text{ cm}^3 = 1 \text{ m}\ell)$.

The metre cubed seen as a cube
and as a cuboid.

Relations between units, multiples,
and submultiples.

The relation $1 \text{m}^3 = 1000 \ \ell$.

Possible link with density.

This is not the only possible order, nor are all possible topics
included, but we suggest that the development keeps in step with the
child's own concepts. Topics not included, such as the area of circles,
are omitted because we consider them more suitable for treatment at
post-primary levels.

The area of a rectangle is a very special case, in that the number of
unit squares can be obtained directly from its length and breadth, if
these are integral. We are surrounded by rectangles, but it is worth
noting that they are all artefacts. Only in a few crystal lattices such as
that of common salt do they fail to signal the work of man. Yet how
often, even in some well defined trade such as glazing, do we in fact
need to know their areas, except to the nearest integer? Floor covering
may be sold by the square unit, but one usually has to buy it in fixed
widths. In spite of all our calculations, we usually finish up with an attic
full of discarded strips.

One feels that the reason so many areas of rectangles have been cal-
culated as exercises is that they are easy to set and mark, they lead to
multiplication of fractions by fractions or decimals by decimals, and
have this spurious suggestion of practical use. It is, of course, an
important configuration and its status as a special case is undeniable,
but it should not be an exercise in decimals. 'Find the area of a rectangle 5·3 cm by 6·4 cm' could be expressed as 'Find the area of a
rectangle 53 mm by 64 mm' and we have no need for the point. The
result in mm^2 can easily be converted to cm^2, although one wonders
why the conversion should be made unless one is going to use the cm^2
specifically. A piece of graph paper shows the pupil that 100 mm^2 =

1 cm², and conversion becomes a matter of understanding the decimal notation. We must add to the four essential number skills listed on page 81:

5.   Multiplication and division of decimal quantities by 10, 100 (and 1000).

and with this the eleven-year old is adequately equipped to deal with the arithmetic of his own world.

Some teachers might like to include work with products such as 5·8 × 2·7, but our own suggestion is that, at least formally, this work should wait till 12+ or beyond. Situations that establish a need for such products can usually be modified by the pupil perhaps with the help of the teacher, so that only one of the numbers is not integral.

The other measures likely to be met in the primary school are of great interest in any discussion of the nature of measurement, but are straightforward matters and do not involve calculation beyond simple integral processes. Of these we first consider angular measure.

Angles

Traditional geometry measures angle in terms of the right angle, the measure of a 'quarter turn'. This is a good starting point for the child, providing he has had earlier experience of angle as turning. He can construct a right angle by folding a sheet of paper twice (it is instructive to do this with an irregularly torn piece rather than a sheet which has four right angled corners anyway) and use it to identify other angles in terms of less than or greater than the standard, and also using very simple fractions such as $\frac{1}{2}$ or $\frac{1}{4}$. This should be an adequate treatment until the child is judged to be capable of using a circular protractor which divides a complete turn into 360°. Note that the concept of angle is dual: there is the static 'corner' where two lines meet, and there is the measure of 'turning'. Both arise naturally if the pupil is given two strips of card pivoted together at one end. It seems much more difficult to move to the dynamic concept if initial stress is laid on the static, so that one suggests that children should turn a strip and 'stop turning' rather than set the strips to a required angle without explicitly noting the movement involved. Some teachers like to bring forward into the primary school the angle and angle-sum properties of polygons, and many children appear to cope with this work. It will almost certainly be repeated and extended by the secondary teacher and can be left, although it is probably worthwhile to explore, by cutting and tearing paper, the angle sum of a triangle and a quadrilateral in terms of right angles and perhaps in degrees. Measures of angles in degrees can be treated arithmetically like lengths, although there are few situations that call for anything beyond multiplication or division by small integers.

Subdivision of the degree will not arise, since children find it difficult (and indeed it *is* difficult) to get an agreed reading to the nearest degree on a small protractor. Bearings, apart from the cardinal points, may well be left till the secondary stage, as well as the conventions of direction in measuring angles and rotation.

For the remaining important measure, temperature, the isomorphism with numbers under the process of addition does not hold and the computation arises in establishing differences of temperature or in rates of change with respect to time. For the purposes of SI units the measure is regarded as fundamental, i.e. is not derived from the other units of mass or length or time.

If then children record temperatures on the Celsius scale and perhaps plot graphs of temperature changes, they are doing all that is needed with this measure. (The Fahrenheit scale is legally obsolete and is better not mentioned in class except in passing).

Time

We work so often with time intervals that we have ceased to think of the activity as computation at all.

'What is the weight of six books if one weighs 230 g?' (needed perhaps if one is sending a parcel of books through the post, but has only a light balance) seems to us a realistic arithmetic example, but 'The cooking time for this dish is 45 mins. It is now 12.12. Where do I set the pinger?' does not seem realistic because the pinger is graduated in minutes from zero. So far we have not found any common uses of clock time (as distinct from elapsed time) that require calculations.

We feel that, if children learn to tell the time—and many do this at home anyway—and become familiar with these day-by-day situations, they are doing all that is needed. Young children do not discriminate

easily between clock time and true time. They feel that to correct a
fast clock just before a TV programme means that they have to wait
longer to hear it! They must, of course, be made familiar with the 24-
hour clock, and be able to record time in all its usual forms. Bus, railway and ferry timetables use exclusively the 24-hour cycle, and all big
stations now have digital rather than dial clocks, working with whole
minute intervals. A model of a digital clock can easily be made with a
card and four strips of paper, and children should be asked to read and
set various times on its face by pulling through the strips (Fig. 15).

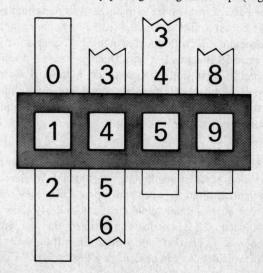

Figure 15

Pure number work can emerge from modular arithmetic with a clock
face as a starting point, as discussed in Chapter 3, but we do not feel
that the work on time should be smothered in complicated calculations.
Such projects as converting Olympic record times into speeds in km/h,
for example, are much more satisfactory for older pupils when a greater
proportion of the class are likely to be able to cope, and will have more
interest in the actual athletics. Shorter intervals of time than the minute
are important and can be handled. One would suggest that all children
should take part in the now familiar classroom activity of setting up a
seconds pendulum. The historical connection of its length with the

metre is interesting. Shorter intervals, of the order of 0·1s, can be seen in action and compared indirectly by reaction time experiments which can easily be done. For example, a child drops a card vertically through the open finger and thumb of another child, who has to stop it as soon as he sees it begin to move. Different children will allow the card to fall different distances and one can order their reaction times, although probably with more fun than precision. The work may usefully be related to reaction times in driving situations.

It will be seen that no new number skills are called for in this work on time. The passage from hours to minutes to seconds implies a sexagesimal base but in fact we use the ten-base system for actually recording time, although with double columns. A sexagesimal base as such would need 59 symbols and zero. One says, '60 s = 1 min', and so 85 s is 1 min 25 s without reference to any notational considerations.

The grasp of the historical time scale comes late in the child's development. It is not specifically related to mathematics, and not at all to computation.

Money

The Decimal Currency Act has deprived the arithmetic teacher of half of his stock-in-trade of manipulative techniques. We have already noted the numerical limits between which practical money transactions within the orbit of the primary child are likely to lie. Because of its suggestion of 'decimals', it is perhaps unfortunate that the term Decimal Currency was used. In context it only means that 100p = £1. In practice, all simple calculations can be done in integers.

> 3 Railway tickets @ £1·32 is the same as
> 3 Railway tickets @ 132p,

and 396p is £3·96. The computation as given seems a satisfactory transitional method for any child having difficulty with decimals.

Although (as suggested on p.72) it is possible to regard cost as a measure of value, we must point out that the actual coinage is not isomorphic with the number system and does not act as a model for it. The notes and coins are arbitrary tokens. The mass : value ratios among the bronze coins does not extend to the nickel coins or the paper notes. In dealing with money, the decimal point is best thought of merely as a separator between the pounds and the pence.

The $\frac{1}{2}$p, of course, is intended to be restricted to the retail trade, and can only occur in practice over a very limited range of computations.

We must also suggest the possibility of introducing children to ready-reckoners. Retailers selling items or unit-priced goods in quantity, like timber merchants or ironmongers, use them extensively, and in our decimal currency they are so simple that children can work out their use for themselves. The unfortunate association between painstaking arithmetic and moral worth has kept this excellent commercial aid out of our classrooms, but one is sure that sufficiently courageous teachers could bring it in. Both using and compiling simple tables are important preparatory steps towards the use of logarithm or trigonometric tables in the secondary school.

6.2 Operation on number

The number operations so far collected as being essential may seem rather thin and restricted. We are not in fact saying that teachers *ought* not to multiply numbers to 2 decimal places by numbers to 2 decimal places, only that they *need* not. We would, however, rather see as many children as possible completely at home with the decimal notation and the number skills between the rough limits we have set out, than a few able children who can cope with extended computation while others fall by the way-side. The able child will acquire these skills anyhow, even if not until the age of 12 or 13, and this is still well before he needs them.

Indeed, and here we are marking a point we regard as vital, too easy a a skill with number often leads to practical nonsense. It is true that $2 \cdot 43 \times 5 \cdot 21 = 12 \cdot 6603$, but if I ask a primary child to calculate the mass of $2 \cdot 43$ cm^3 of a substance if each cm^3 weighs $5 \cdot 21$ g and he triumphantly produces the result $12 \cdot 6603$ g, then he is producing nonsense. We think it is too difficult for most children to realize why it is nonsense, and indeed it is often difficult to convince an adult that $12 \cdot 6571$, say, would be equally correct or incorrect. The best way is to avoid the problem of significant figures by avoiding questions that raise it. We want numerical skills to keep pace with the need for them in handling practical problems. But many practical problems also involve conceptual difficulties that only older and maturer pupils can begin to grasp, and to develop numerical skills as such on the assumption that they are sufficient in themselves, is to make nonsense of the practical approach to arithmetic that is typical of English education.

Appendix 1

Reference points for thinking metric

Most adults and many older children have already a rough idea of a foot, a yard, a pound—even if such pastimes as 'guessing the weight of the cake' show that it is often rougher than we imagine.

It is now essential for us to have a similar rough idea of the metric measures, and here is a typical list of common objects measured in rounded-off metric units, within the limits of the average person's ability to discriminate. Children should certainly not be set to learn such a list, but work with units will enable them to construct their own references. The list might be of value to teachers.

Mass

2 brass drawing pins	1 g
Stick of chalk	10 g
Packet of tea (¼ lb. + package)	100 g
Large packet of sugar (2 lb. + package)	1 kg
1 ton of coal	1 Mg = 1000 kg
(This measure is the metric tonne)	
Adult (female)	50 kg and upwards
(male)	75 kg and upwards

Weight (on Earth)

Large packet of sugar	10 N
One medium apple	1 N
(These measures are given for the teacher: the use of the newton is inappropriate for primary schools)	

Length

Width of 3p stamp	2 cm
Width of 50p coin	3 cm
Height of door	2 m
Cricket pitch	20 m
Straits of Dover	35 km
London to Hastings, Bognor, Colchester, or Oxford	100 km
A 15-minute stroll might be about the distance represented by a grid interval on an O.S. one inch map	1 km

Area

Cross section of butt end of a stick of chalk	1 cm^2
Large door	2 m^2
Full-sized football pitch	$1 \text{ ha} = 10\,000 \text{ m}^2$

Volume and capacity

Cherry stone	1 cm^3
Unit in Cuisenaire or Color Factor Apparatus	1 cm^3
Medicine spoon	$5 \text{ m}\ell$
Saucepan (2 pt, nearly full)	1ℓ
Orange Squash (35 fl. oz)	1ℓ

Movement

Brisk walk	5 km/h
Speed limits (30 mph)	50 km/h
(70 mph)	120 km/h

(These last two are the nearest rounded values)

Temperature

Freezing	$0\,^\circ\text{C}$
Cool day	$10\,^\circ\text{C}$
Warm day	$20\,^\circ\text{C}$
Normal body temperature	$37\,^\circ\text{C}$
Boiling water	$100\,^\circ\text{C}$

Appendix 2

Summary of the SI measures as required at primary level

The Système Internationale (SI) units, are based on the original metric system, but are not identical with it. Only four of the seven basic units (SI) will be generally used outside science and technology.

Measure	Unit	Symbol
Length	metre	m
Mass	kilogram	kg
Time	second	s
Temperature	kelvin	K

For all ordinary purposes, the interval of one kelvin is the same as the interval one degree Celsius (Centigrade). The zero points are different, i.e. $0\,^\circ\text{C} = 273$ K. In schools the $^\circ\text{C}$ will be used. There are two other standard derived units which will be needed:

Measure	Unit	Symbol
Area	square metre	m^2
Volume	cubic metre	m^3

There are also 'customary units', not formally part of the system, but needed for everyday practical measurement:

Fluid capacity	–	litre (ℓ)
Angle	–	degree ($^\circ$)
Land Measure	–	hectare (ha)
(1 ha = 10 000 m^2)		(1 000 ℓ = 1 m^3)

To these will be added the usual units of time (hours, years, etc.) Apart from the special needs of science and technology, the full range of measures required in schools and for general purposes is restricted to the following multiples and sub-multiples.

Length	Mass ('Weight')	Area
kilometre (km)	kilogram (kg)	square metre (m^2)
metre (m)	gram (g)	square centimetre (cm^2)
decimetre (dm)		
centimetre (cm)	milligram (mg)	square millimetre (mm^2)
millimetre (mm)		hectare (ha)

Volume	Fluid capacity	Time
cubic metre (m^3)	litre (ℓ)	All common units
cubic centimetre (cm^3)	millilitre ($m\ell$)	
cubic millimetre (mm^3)		

Of these, the centimetre and the decimetre are not formally recommended but will be needed as teaching measures and are better not subdivided. If sub-division is required, use a smaller unit, e.g. 123 mm not 12·3 cm.

Reference may be made to publications such as the Royal Society's *Metric Units for Primary Schools*, for suggestions on useful equipment to help familiarization with metric units.

CHAPTER SEVEN

SPATIAL AND NON-ARITHMETICAL CONCEPTS

The movement which began with Descartes' transformation of problems in geometry to exercises in algebra and which finished in the programme to 'arithmetize' the whole of mathematics can, for those familiar with the subject, hide the clear psychological distinctions between numerical operations and spatial concepts. The early books of Euclid are completely non-numerical, developing each statement fully in words. It was not until the alternative formulations at the end of the nineteenth century that the more economical use of symbols was permitted. Even then, arithmetic, algebra, and geometry remained almost unrelated, and had separate textbooks, separate lessons, separate examinations and in some secondary schools, separate teachers.

Although one would not defend this today, the move towards a unified approach (signalled after the Jeffery Report of 1941 by the appearance of textbooks in which the distinctions were reduced to separate chapters in volumes on general mathematics) may obscure the pedagogic differences for the sake of the logical unity.

For primary children, at least, spatial concepts can develop irrespective of numerical ones. Older people whose mathematics as small children was entirely restricted to numerical calculations can sometimes remember the pleasure and relief with which they first met geometry.

For all that, mathematics *can* be presented as a unified study and we think that teachers should be aware of this possibility. But at the children's level, the work in non-numerical mathematics should be left rather loose, and should be connected only where the connections are obvious. What is important, we suggest, is that the children get a rich and varied set of experiences which will at some later stage cohere into mathematics. Thus, we would hope that in their activities they would handle all the isometries of the plane, but we would not expect an attempt to be made to formulate the generalized concept that the phrase implies. Children working in this way may well arrive at a generalized insight, but this is a quite different matter.

This set of experiences, based on handling and discussing shapes, structures, and situations which are mathematical but call for no skill in computation, should be as wide as the child's own interests and abilities allow. It is a great temptation to arrange these experiences into a recommended order, to attach age ranges to such skills as tessellation or curve-stitching and to impose progression on them. But in fact, they are all, or nearly all, applicable at each level in some form or another. We have, however, attempted a rough grading in terms of a passage through first and middle schools. Some of the work commonly met in primary schools is an informal presentation of the secondary geometry of an earlier generation, and sometimes topics one meets in lists of activities only give names to what toddlers may already know how to do. Consider, for example, tessellation. The pre-school child who can pack his building blocks back into the box is tessellating, but the word now carries all the overtones of a systematic mathematical investigation and we can extend it in this way. A bathroom tile is square or rectangular for convenience, but what shapes could it be if there were no production difficulties? It is possible to give an exact mathematical formulation of the possibilities, roughly at the level appropriate to a sixth-former, and he, too, is then investigating tessel-ation. Between these levels is a whole gamut of activity and investigation Perhaps we may note in passing the great difficulty some ten-year olds have in copying a repeat pattern in successive squares. This suggests children may lack the basic experiences.

In suggesting lists of topics, we have tried to show how far they should usually be taken in the primary school, but we have not tried to avoid technical terms on the grounds that they appear more at home in A-level syllabuses. Here as always, the teacher's own skill and judge-ment decides what is done. We only recall the reference to the use of language in Chapter 5. Although no attempt is made to define an order within each group, it is clear that certain items are necessarily connected and show a natural progression.

7.1   Development of spatial concepts at Infant level

Spatial concepts not involving measure and distance—topological concepts in other words—seem to develop first. The work will need to be based on much discussion and handling of objects in a variety of ways. Much of the language will be developed in creative work such as modelling or in Wendy-house play. More formally, we shall have:

1. Recognition, handling and naming of the shapes square, circle, triangle, ball, and block, with the associated descriptive vocabulary of words such as straight, curved, round, flat, thick, thin.

2. The recognition of pictures and diagrams representing the shapes met and handled, and early attempts to draw them in colour and in line.

3. Matching and ordering according to size and shape, colour, texture, etc. There must be a distinction between sorting into sets and ordering within a set.

4. Recognition of shapes in the environment of the classroom, for example in the Wendy house, the percussion band, cooking utensils, tools.

5. Larger scale activities, such as running or walking round circles, squares and triangles, either drawn in the playground or imagined as in drama.

6. The usual play with sand, water and clay, the experience of cutting out, constructional toys and apparatus.

7. The shapes handled, named and recognized should by now be including rectangle, hexagon, cone, cylinder and cube; again with associated descriptive words and phrases.

8. More extended work in shapes such as simple tessellation (with polygons supplied ready cut) patterns with shapes in colour, matching and covering of shapes, sorting into 'same and different' using as many criteria as possible.

9. Vocabulary recognition in print and writing, with initial stages of recording (e.g. 'My Book of Triangles')

The importance of the mathematical topics in extending vocabulary must be stressed. The initial vocabulary of the standard first readers has often been criticized. Here is an opportunity to introduce words in a context of activity. The sentence 'This is a cow' may well be met by a child who has never seen one, but every child can handle, draw, cut out, colour or collect 'triangles'.

Of these topics, number 2 on the use and recognition of pictures and diagrams is very interesting pedagogically. We are so used to them that we regard a picture as self-explanatory, yet children brought up entirely without them, as formerly among desert tribes of strict Muslim Arabs, are said to be unable to recognize the two-dimensional conventions by which we represent a solid object. Deaf children also find these difficulties, because they miss the verbal commentary that, for the normal child, accompanies his visual experiences. And certainly the diagram, as distinct from the picture, is a convention that needs to be learned. This is particularly true of scientific diagrams. Secondary teachers of wood- or metal-work report that many less able children fail to progress, not because they lack manual skills, but because they cannot read the drawings, or see in their minds the solid represented by the plane configuration of lines. It would seem that the use of the diagram should begin as early as possible, and should be developed consistently throughout the first stages of schooling.

7.2   Work with Lower Juniors

At this stage there is an attempt to extend the topics already encountered in a more systematic way. Examples of the development would be

1. Extension of 'square corner' to 'right angle'.
2. Classification of triangles as right angled, equilateral, and others.
3. Regular and irregular polygons made with straws or drawn with templates, explored as possible units in a tessellation.
4. Noting the rigidity of the triangular frame compared with the flexibility of all other polygons, and its consequent use in engineering and other structures.
5. Extension of bilateral symmetry from initial experience with ink blots, to more complicated paper folding and cutting.
6. Introduction to rotational symmetry.
7. Three dimensional models by paper folding (origami).
8. Patterns by curve stitching.
9. Exploration of the ways of fitting plane shapes into frames and solids into fitted boxes.

It should be seen that at this stage, topics are beginning to open up and remain capable of extensive development at secondary levels or beyond. It is this potential for development that characterizes many of the topics of the newer mathematics teaching, and it is of help if the teacher is aware of these possibilities. Thus, at this stage, we merely note that the triangular linkage is rigid, while 4, 5, 6, . . . n-sided polygons are not. At a much later stage, one discusses the possible movements of various polygons, with special reference to the four-bar linkages whose motion geometry is important throughout the entire field of mechanical engineering.

Similarly, we note at primary level only the pleasing patterns produced by curve stitching; but very few of our pupils will go on to investigate the mathematics of these envelope curves. Many of the above ideas are generated by work with dissected puzzles.

7.3   Later work with Juniors

At this stage, we feel that it is difficult to maintain the necessary informal approach, although open-ended discussions are by now becoming very fruitful. Lists of topics now begin to include terms such as 'parallel', 'coordinates', and so on; and because we are now using the normal vocabulary of mathematics, there is a danger of a formal mathematical treatment.

Here are some of the topics that could be covered at this level:

1. Further work with angle. (Since we *measure* angles, this topic has already been discussed in Chapter 6 ('Number in action'). The words obtuse and acute must be known, and the angle sum of the triangle and the quadrilateral by tearing off the corners could probably be done.

2. Parallels and gradients—a practical approach via railway lines, roads, and sloping structures, avoiding anything approaching the parallel line theorems of Euclid, or attempts to quantify gradient except in informal discussion of road gradients.

3. Coordinates as records of position, through use of squared paper for treasure hunt games and so on. They can be seen as related to the numbers at the edges of maps.

4. The concept of similarity through enlargement and reduction, and the first steps towards its quantification as scale.

One notes here the interesting case of road gradient. Through road signs, if less frequently now through railway gradients, the measure of slope has become quite familiar to many children, who know that 1 in 8 is steeper than 1 in 10. It is one of the many examples where the outside world has caught up and passed the traditional school course, in which gradient was not treated until the fourth year of a grammar school.

7.4   Development of concepts among Top Juniors or early in the Middle School

The main characteristic of the work at this level is the gradual quantification of the child's spatial concepts, the link-up with the number skills we still think of as arithmetic. The non-numerical topics continue to be extended and are of undiminished importance, but they are now accompanied by more systematic work. At this stage, too, the topics tend to be selective: there is so much that can be done that the teacher is faced with a choice. The topics listed are among the more important of those available.

1.   A more formal treatment of coordinates with introduction of x- and y-axes and graphs. These would be in the positive quadrant, and mainly but not exclusively linear.
2.   The Pythagoras relationship for 3 : 4 : 5 and a few other triangles, treated both numerically and by dissection.
3.   Height finding, using clinometers and scale drawing.
4.   Scale drawing of simple configurations.
5.   A more systematic discussion of symmetry—lines of symmetry. The translation, rotation, and reflection of simple shapes, using templates, plane tracing paper, and mirrors. Patterns made by these transformations.
6.   Pattern making with compasses and set squares.
7.   The construction of plane nets to form polyhedra.
8.   Informal treatment of circumference: diameter ratio of circle.

It will be seen that this list does not contain much 'modern' material. We feel that in mathematics as in other subjects, it is always worthwhile to keep back some good wine. Whether primary pupils transfer to a middle or a secondary school, it does help if some new topics can be produced at that level. Given skilful teaching, primary children may well be able to grasp the principles of plane table surveying, of the use of vector quantities, or the first ideas of topology. But we think it not only fairer to the secondary teacher not to have given an elementary introduction to everything on a modern General Certificate syllabus, but fairer to the topics themselves to leave some of them to maturer skills. One does, for example, find beautifully executed plane table surveys done by secondary children, which are far beyond the reach of the more happy-go-lucky skills of the junior. It must be a great help to a teacher, keen and well informed on this or any similar topic, to find that he can begin from scratch with the initial motivation of novelty.

This is not to deny a junior child the opportunity of investigating anything the teacher considers appropriate, but we do suggest that such topics are not laid down as class projects to be done each year as part of a work scheme. As we suggest later, it would be of great value if some record of what had been done went with the child as he moves on from the first school.

7.5   Other mathematical situations: games

One often feels that the old trio of arithmetic, algebra and geometry, by imposing a classification on school mathematics, squeezed out many topics and activities because they did not fit in with the tripartite scheme. An example at secondary level is that of vectors, which a generation ago only appeared in a setting of mechanics. Another interesting field for our purpose is that of board or table games. Could chess and draughts be activities subsumed under a mathematics scheme? Clearly this is so at a suitably advanced level. A game of pure chance such as snakes and ladders can be analysed in terms of probabilities and we can ask (and, indeed answer mathematically) the question 'If one move is made each minute, what is the probable average duration of a large number of games of snakes and ladders?'

At the other extreme, for a game of almost pure strategy such as chess, one can ask 'What is the probable best move to make in the circumstances?' This question seems to be so close to the one asked in mathematics 'What is the next step I ought to take to proceed with solving this problem?' that one expects to find a link.

What we are suggesting is that, in a primary school, certain games of skill or chance can be played as part of the educational programme, particularly if the teacher is aware of their basis in mathematics and can ask children the right questions. To set a pair of children to play snakes and ladders, and afterwards to ask them to write down the numbers of all the squares that could possibly be occupied after

(1)   one throw each,
(2)   two throws each,

leads directly to overtly mathematical thinking at a very high level.

An excellent example of a game of educational value is given by dominoes. It has a simple rule of play which is easily grasped by children, yet calls for a definite strategy whereby one can block the move of an opponent. The process of eliminating possibilities and arriving at a final choice of pieces to be played is clearly analogous to finding a step in a proof.

It is easy to see what games are and what are not suitable. Monopoly and similar group games, although they involve much mental arithmetic, are too long winded and loosely structured to be of educational value in school, although they can probably contribute at home.

It is the short compact games, from the humble noughts and crosses up through ludo and halma to draughts and the large variety of peg-board games that can be constructed, that seem to offer the best opportunities. Many apparently simple but subtly structured situations exist in the form of commercial puzzles and games, and there are special games such as Battleships that require logical thinking based on what has gone before.

We would suggest that teachers should consider to what extent such activities can legitimately and with educational profit be encouraged in classrooms. We recommend those who have not yet met them to explore the peg-board games in Tahta's booklet [1].

7.6   The mathematics of movement

Although we are surrounded by movement, the actual mathematical analysis of movement, the distinctions, kinetic and kinematic, between translation, rotation, and circulation, between uniform and accelerated motion, is by no means simple. In primary schools, one approaches it only through chosen straightforward examples, and even here only quantifying in the simplest of them. One would mention accelerated motion in discussion, but one would only suggest calculation for uniform motion, and note that the concept of speed is less simple than it seems. One would also note revolution as fast or slow, perhaps using revolutions per minute, but no attempt would be made to discuss angular velocity.

We suggest that as many movements as possible should be observed and discussed in qualitative terms, so that the pupil becomes familiar with them and is able later to give numerical expression to them. For most children this familiarity arises outside the school environment. To fill in gaps and to help the less fortunate child, the school should have available, as models or in actuality, examples of movements such as these:

—Movement of screws, nuts, and bolts
—Gear trains
—Gramophone turntable
—Movement of ladders and poles during erection
—Tools involving turning or twisting (hand-drills, gimlets, etc.)
—Wheels and rollers
—Movements in the bicycle
—Acceleration down a slope
—Motion in a circle—including centrifugal effects and vortices
—Acceleration of large and small masses
—Compound movements such as the 'Spirograph' toy
—Lever action
—Construction kits or models for cranes, diggers, hoists, and the like.

We do not recommend that any of these should be made an excuse for calculation, only that the child should investigate, or if necessary, have his attention drawn to, the sort of movements that occur. One would compare the working of the mechanism with the purpose it serves, and might even attempt a classification according to type of motion.

Reference

[1] R. Tahta, *Pegboard games*, Association of Teachers of Mathematics, 1967.

CHAPTER EIGHT

THE DEVELOPMENT OF GRAPHICAL REPRESENTATION

It is not so long ago that the sight of a graph on the wall of a primary classroom would have called for comment if not for surprise. Today the surprise would more surely be felt, even in an Infant room, if there were no graph on the walls. At the same time, the body of work that has come to be called Graph Theory has, superficially at least, little to do with graphs as they are generally understood in primary schools. Increasing use in mathematics is now made of the visual representation of relationships of a non-numerical rather than a metrical nature, and it is the study of this diagrammatic expression of relations and its great variety of applications which is now developed in the topic of Graph Theory.

The graph itself is any one of many forms of visual representation. It is this introduction of the visual element to help in developing abstract ideas which has made the form so acceptable to many teachers at first school levels.

We can detect three stages in the development of graphs in the primary school, though we must stress that these stages merge into one another rather than show clear cut distinctions. They must, like all other developments of mathematical work, follow the mental growth of the children concerned and not be tied to ages, class levels, or any other chronological yardstick.

The first stage could be called that of random approach. Here the important characteristics are as follows:

1. Activity as a group experience to parallel the individual work in classifying, sorting, and matching, and to be a logical extension of their vocabulary.
2. The concrete nature of the experience, using in the work everyday objects like beads, small jars, cubes, coins, and (less common today) matchboxes.

3. The link that these everyday objects provide with the home environment, helping to establish the notion that mathematics *is* concerned with ordinary life and is *not* an utterly separate activity only for the classroom.

4. The active approach to graphical representation. It does not matter in the least from the mathematical point of view what specific activity is chosen. The young child may first cover a matchbox with paper of a colour to match his jersey and put it, duly named, on the appropriate pile. He may arrange his shoes within a circle, as described in Chapter 1. He may thread beads on a string to match the number of cows or horses in his toy farmyard, or make a tower of plastic interlock cubes to compare the different makes of toy motor cars in his possession, or link with strands of wool corresponding items in a pair of sets. Later, when his skill permits, he may make a plasticine model of his parents standing behind little figures to represent his brothers and sisters (and himself, if he remembers!)

Eventually we come to such things as rows of pennies (commercial plastic coins are useful here) matching the price of various sweet packages mounted beside them, and at this stage the combination of concepts, the degree of abstraction, and the size of the numbers involved begin to demand more typically mathematical thinking.

Meanwhile we have, in the rows of objects or columns of beads, the essential ideas of the bar chart, in the circle formation the introduction to the pie-chart, in the arrangement of the model of his family the basis of a network or tree. The latter helps, too, his understanding of the natural growth of trees with their repeated branching, replacing his early idea of a simple two-part structure of solid trunk and brush-like top. His sets connected with lines of wool foreshadow mapping diagrams, and the overlapping sets he soon encounters, bounded by hoops, cords, coloured papers, or whatever, will later develop into Venn diagrams with little trouble.

Corresponding to the rapid changes of interest of most children at the Infant stage, these early graphical forms are all transitory in nature, and the same objects will be used again and again for a variety of purposes—many of them not mathematical at all. Sooner or later the desire to make some more permanent record arises. It is with this urge for a longer-lasting or permanent form of presentation that we move on to the next stage. Here real objects such as pennies or bottle tops are mounted on paper, followed first by pictures of them and then by symbols. Before long even the simplified isotype symbols give way to abstract crosses or dots, and these in turn to coloured bars and finally to the abstraction of 'space up to', the top of the bar only being marked. We would note that at first the square, so convenient for adults, should be avoided as a symbol. The way squares run into each other and form a bar may hide from the young mathematician the discrete nature of the items represented by the set of squares forming a single bar. Eventually we think of them as a single bar or column, but at first we need to keep the representation discrete.

With the extension of graphical work from real objects to representation on paper, we move firmly into the second stage which we have already called the helical approach stage. The theory behind this approach is discussed in general terms in Chapter 2. Here we link it with the variability principle, by which an abstract idea is presented in a variety of forms and contexts, using many materials and situations. From these the learner may come to comprehend the common elements and so develop the abstract idea behind the forms and situations. Applying this principle to the early graphical concepts, we see two main ways in which we can introduce this variability. First, we use the same situation to provide numerical information which we portray in the same way but with different materials, or in a variety of graphical forms. Secondly, we use the same materials and the same graphical forms to portray the information arising in a variety of situations. Always there should be a discussion of the activity. The children could be led to an evaluation at first in very simple terms of both the form used and the actual results shown. Always too, the graphs should arise naturally from other work—graphs are not an end in themselves but a way of displaying and comparing information. They make the information more easily assimilated, demonstrate relationships such as linearity, and suggest possibilities of further investigation. As the helical approach is applied to other aspects of work, so too will opportunities for graphs come round again and again; as the situations recur, so also will the increase in sophistication of methods of representation.

When the children have advanced to the use of squared paper and number relations begin to predominate, we proceed from the actual numbers corresponding to the number of squares, to the use of a scale. This implies more complex thinking with the use of a false origin (i.e. not starting the labelling of the axes at zero) or the use of different scales on the two axes, until at secondary stages one approaches the use of non-linear scales such as log scales. Meanwhile there is gradually increased stress on the more abstract network and relational graphs, on the relationship between the coordinates, and a development towards algebraic and trigonometrical graphs. Similarly bar charts progress from their first simple forms to situations which show the effects of combining information. We refer to the earlier situation where addition was met as a process operating on collections of objects, and care had to be taken to add only items which were compatible. Now the children must consider what types of information are compatible for combination in one compound bar chart and what must be represented separately. This is a step of fundamental importance. Pie-charts, too, will develop from their first heuristic setting (see Chapter 1) through the use of tracing paper and folding methods for clock angles, e.g. for times spent in various activities in hours of the day or months of the year. Finally we reach more abstract divisions of the complete turn in simple fractions of right-angles and eventually in degrees.

Parallel to the increase in complexity of both forms of representation and the situation involved, there will have been deeper consideration of the labelling of the graph. Most of the early graphs at the infant stage will not need labelling as the children *know* what they are about (and are only too anxious to tell any new comer to the group all about it).

However, the practice of labelling most things on display helps with the learning of reading and the teacher will undoubtedly discuss labels with the group. The onus of labelling thus moves steadily from teacher to the makers of the graph, from the purpose of the label as an aid to reading to that of assisting communication with someone who does not previously know what it is all about. We move gradually from 'what we can say about it' to more conventional forms of labelling.

We come now to the third stage of approach to graphical work, when the children are already familiar with a variety of forms of representation both graphical and otherwise, when they have had some experience in

comparing different forms in different situations and in drawing conclusions from them. In this stage, topics may well be developed through
graphs, or graphs through topics, in a more linear fashion, with these
topics running either in parallel or in series. The earlier work will now
be more systematized, points originally made in passing will be reviewed
and finer shades of development in different situations noticed. For
example, in the early work on pie-charts the children are simply aware
of sectors as parts of the whole circle—the basic idea of this form of
introductory presentation. Through the helical approach the idea of
angles will have been met, first as a measure of turning, then in a
static sense as the size of a corner arising from paper folding and the
use of tracing paper. These notions come together with an operational
understanding of fractions in the more sophisticated pie-chart where
calculations are made to within a degree and careful consideration is
given to the radii chosen. The effects of the sequence of positions round
the circle and the details of the labelling also require discussion. With
the gradually maturing understanding of the continuity and intervals of
time, we have the increase in significance of time-charts, with longer
time-spans becoming meaningful. We bear in mind the experience of
teachers and the work of psychologists, which shows that many
Reception children barely understand 'yesterday' and 'tomorrow', and
that not until about nine or ten years old is there any real appreciation
of the time-span of a year. We suggest flow charts evolving from a series
of pictures of sequences (like baby, child, grown-up, old man) or
biological cycles like

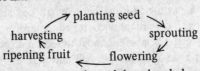

or the development of insects through larval and chrysalid stages. An
example less immediately connected with the child's observation would
be the set of processes from the writing of a letter, its treatment in the
post office network to its eventual arrival and perusal. Yet another is
the break-down of a familiar numerical algorithm into its basic steps
prior to its application in a new or extended realm. We have now reached
a sophisticated level of operation.

Simple mapping diagrams may show two distinct lines of development: non-metric situations lending themselves to graphs of relations and so to simple network theory, and situations leading to statistical or algebraic graphs. Much has been written elsewhere about these types of representation, so here we are content with only four comments. First, we think it undesirable to introduce children too exclusively to so many straight-line graphs at once that they lose the sense of satisfaction felt on discovering the existence of a simple linear relationship. Secondly, it seems a pity to use the term histogram for column graphs where only the height of columns is important since they are all of the same width. It is only when we use columns of different widths—as in the numbers of a population in varying age groups—that we bring out the correct definition of the histogram as the display of the frequency of the groups by proportional areas.

Thirdly, care needs to be taken that technical problems, such as scaling or the difficulties of estimating subdivisions, do not inhibit the appreciation of the basic idea of a graph.

Lastly, the use of simple scattergrams provides another means of looking for relationships. It offers scope for appreciation of the importance of discriminating between a fortuitous correlation on the one hand and a direct or indirect causal connection on the other.

To conclude this brief report of graphical work, we note some of the mathematical bonuses obtained besides the learning points mentioned above.

1. There are useful opportunities while practising graphical representation to gain added insight into some features of the social or natural environment, perhaps by exploring the idea of randomness or some of the biologically important notions like dominance and deviation. Graphs of shoe sizes, oral temperature, and height show significant examples of the deviations among a population, and a measure such as standing height may be compared with sitting height. All could be related to commercial and social problems like the stock a shopkeeper needs, or when to call the doctor. If a teacher is sufficiently confident to be able to process the material to the interests of a primary class, he will find that biological dominance offers a wide field of possibility. It may be explored for

example through eye-colour, the characteristics of free ear-lobes or crooked middle fingers. The proportion of tongue-rollers to others is interesting and easily recorded. Sweet-tasting (at various concentrations of sugar, say from 0·001 per cent by weight in water up to 0·5 per cent) provides a cumulative frequency diagram of scientific as well as mathematical significance.

2. Reading and recording results and the experience of scaling the values obtained are likely to contribute to the understanding of approximation, tolerances, and the inherent limitations of measurement.

3. As a joint creation requiring personal discipline and seen as complementary to the freer cooperation required in making such things as collage, the completion and use of a graph promotes a most satisfying sense of achievement for members of a group.

4. At all stages, and especially in the early years of school life where oral work is so vital, graphs provide a productive basis for group discussion. Later they remain important in promoting among pupils both the use and the interpretation of mathematical language and symbolism of varied kinds.

5. The progress through the stages of graphical work as suggested above leads steadily from manipulation of objects in the three dimensional world of visual symbols represented on the plane of a sheet of paper, to the abstract world of the mathematician. Professor Sawyer believes that 'one main task of primary school work is to effect a smooth transition from arithmetic to algebra'. We suggest the progressive experiences of a variety of graphical work can help realize this aim.

6. Graph work encourages pupils to discuss the effectiveness, for some particular purpose, of different methods available to him. The opportunity to make visual comparisons, to discuss the validity of results read from different forms of representation, and to check the impressions produced by them, all develops insight into how 'altering the rules changes the game' and generates confidence in the choice of representation actually made. The attitudes developed will later be of great importance in more abstract work.

7. Reflection on his experience of graphical work can by analogy clarify, for the older child, the evolutionary nature of arrival at

conventional techniques: symbols gain depth of meaning as they gradually supplant physical manipulations, and processes are discarded as they are outgrown. What replaces them tends to be more abstract.

8. Pictorial representation, and graphical work in general, provides a linking factor, enabling a child to get early experience of what he will later find again in other topics as the underlying unity of the diversity we see in mathematics.

These we have called bonuses, but they will only be received in full if at appropriate stages the relevant points are made explicitly, and this in turn will only happen if the teacher has already become aware of the possibilities and is alert for opportunities to cultivate them. We must also appreciate the great importance of developing the child's ability to comprehend matter presented either verbally, or visually, or in specifically mathematical language. Given these prerequisites, we feel that work of the nature discussed in this chapter contributes towards fulfilling the educational function of the primary school. We saw as the function of the school the responsibility for:

1. Giving experiences, on which systematization may be built.
2. Teaching the language—both verbal and visual—in terms of which such systematization may take place.
3. Providing the firm motivation for further development and an emotional attitude such that the child's energies may be harnessed for these purposes.
4. Socializing by developing powers of working together and of facility in communication.

Clearly these functions go beyond the teaching of mathematics. We do, however, suggest that the work on graphs makes a direct and obvious contribution.

CHAPTER NINE

MATHEMATICS AND THE SUCCESS OF THE TEACHER

Whether one regrets it or accepts it as inevitable, the teaching of mathematics at school seems inextricably tied up with assessment, even if this is nothing more than reading out the answers to a set of examples worked in class. Moreover, parents or head-teachers often demand that the new methods and content should allow for assessment.

The first stages in a learning programme should set the levels of the actual objectives, and assessment as such is only to help one judge if these levels are being attained. It is also tied up with a general educational aim, which may set standards of achievement for mathematics only as one of several contributory factors. We shall suggest possible aims for assessment and comment on them.

It is, of course, possible to give a lesson or lecture, set a test on the work covered and record the result as an assessment of learning on the part of the pupil. We assume that we all have in mind something more educationally useful than this, and make our comments accordingly.

9.1 Aims of Assessment

One aim of assessment is to provide information for *modifying the learning situation*, by checking the success of what is being done at suitable stages in the process. The teacher herself has control over the teaching situation, and it is through this that she affects the learning situation in which the children are placed. Assessment should show whether this situation is effective, and help the teacher to change it if is not. The teacher has to decide both on her objectives and her methods, and assessment helps her to judge the attainment of the one and the efficiency of the other. It also helps a teacher when she has to take over from another.

In so far as the teacher does this for herself in her own class, this aim can be realized, but we now have an almost unresolved problem in education, in that any form of assessment which attempts external and objective standards tends to dictate not only what is taught, but how it is taught. This is particularly true at primary level, with Common Entrance or Selection Tests, which may result in the widespread retention of fossilized topics and the rejection of new ones, not for arguable educational reasons but merely because they are in or not in the tests. Fortunately, it is now true that examination syllabuses and schedules are being modified to meet present-day needs and a machinery is developing over which teachers, if they will, can have some sort of control, although the dialectics of the process are still very one-sided. Some local authorities are content to employ standard tests as published.

We shall take it, however, that no teacher actively wishes an assessment procedure, internal or external, to dominate the classroom situation or to be an end in itself.

One of the functions of assessment is to ensure progression. It is part of the programme of developing a topic, marking the point at which another stage is started. In this way it remains itself part of the teaching method. If it is a time-consuming activity removed from the development of the subject, like the usual end of term examinations in many secondary schools, then it may be failing in this educational function.

Assessment must also be significant for the child. It should provide the pupil with a knowledge of results and progress, but should not appear as a once and for all judgement of work done over a long period. In other words, if a progression is to be maintained it should be assessed at each stage, in steps whose size is adjusted to the abilities of the child to avoid as far as possible the fear of present or ultimate failure.

This appears to be a key use of assessment and testing. If no progress is made through the early stages of a topic, then there is no point, as far as the pupil is concerned, in pressing on regardless of failure. Many primary teachers intuitively use this day by day mode of assessment already—it is at higher levels that the hurdle nature of examinations becomes more apparent.

If assessment is used comprehensively, it becomes much more clearly part of the teaching and learning processes, is parallel with them and, like them, is adapted to the immediate situation as the teacher sees it. Instead of depressing the child, it can encourage him to progress and to overcome his difficulties, and it can give him an active involvement in the progression of his learning, rather than leave him a passive absorber of information.

Not only should assessment help both child and teacher in the immediate learning situation, it should, at least within a school but ideally from school to school, provide a continuity of learning. This should be more efficient than a process of dividing up a total syllabus into one-year sections—although primary schools have already moved well away from this fragmented teaching. Where a school can organize this assessment without its becoming an end in itself, then there is long-term security for the child in spite of staff changes and the growth of new topics and methods.

This feeling of continuity is certainly as important for the teacher as for the child. She wants to know that there is a programme capable of assessment and evaluation and that within this programme progression of learning is in fact taking place. She should at least be able to compare her work with others within the school. If she could do it outside her own school, it would give further reassurance, both for teacher and school. It might do much to remove the professional isolation of the teacher in her classroom.

Assessment also has a practical external function. It can be used by Heads and teachers in discussing both school policy and individual progress, among themselves or with parents. This is particularly true if new methods or new content are at issue.

Internally, assessment is diagnostic if properly used. It can enable us to determine a child's readiness to follow a particular route or to select one of several routes available. Clearly, if it is to be used this way, it must be much more than a percentage mark, and the test material needs to be very carefully devised, although we stress once again that it may be dangerous to use it to replace the teacher's own skills in deciding a child's needs. The good teacher cannot abdicate this responsibility.

Finally, external assessment is undoubtedly a means of comparing results in one school with a wider population. It is not, however, always clear *why* this comparison needs to be made. If the wider population were homogeneous, it could probably demonstrate the efficiency of a school, but extending the locale often brings in groups of different educational needs and largely different backgrounds, and the carefully turned 'objective' test may tend to pick up and record in terms of gradings or marks, vastly different and subjectively uncomparable factors.

9.2   Forms of Assessment

The distinction made between objective and subjective assessments reflects an attitude as much as a technique. There are those for whom the word 'subjective' is equivalent to unreliable, and there are those for whom 'objective' stands for a form of self-deceit. No doubt any practicable test has aspects of both. We must also reckon that testing will differ according to its basic purpose, which will be either to assess whether a minimum level regarded as essential has been reached, or to decide the developmental level achieved at the time of testing. We can, for convenience, distinguish

1. *Assessment by work done*   Here we mean, not special tests, but the keeping of selections of the child's work, made either by the teacher or the child, or both, and the recording against a check list of topics satisfactorily completed.
2. *Records of self-evaluation*   This is most important, and increasingly so in current educational thinking. The teacher needs to organize the situation so that the self-evaluation takes place. This is not easy to do, since it must be made within the capacity of the child to make the necessary decisions. Children themselves can keep check lists of topics, or the work of one may check that of another, and there are many possible self-checking activities, or activities whose outcome can be seen by the teacher at a glance.
3. *Individual or group assessment*   Here we mean the actual marking of work, either set as part of the development of a topic, or as a special test at some intermediate or final stage. Nowadays individual assessment will be used as far as possible, based perhaps on the child's completion of a work card. This may be a special test-card or his resolution of a problem situation set for him by the teacher The group or formal class test can sometimes be of value in providing an overall check, but one hopes that today in the primary school it would not be used to put the children into order of ability or achievement. Such an order is at the best impermanent and can

be both misleading and disencouraging.

4. *Internal and external assessment*   The internal methods are those mentioned in 3 above which originate with a teacher. One can, however, use externally devised tests such as the Nuffield *Checkups* or the NFER tests. These, because of the work and evaluation that have gone into producing them, have a greater objective validity in general, providing, of course, that they are appropriate and applicable to the situation in which they are used. One must appreciate that this validity only applies to the purposes for which they have been designed and tested. One must also distinguish sharply between such external tests used within a class for its own purposes in assessing progress or deciding a strategy, and those imposed on the school from without for such purposes as secondary selection. It is at this point that they begin to influence the work done by the children.

5. *Explicit and incidental testing*   The distinction is important. If work is set as part of the development of a topic, but is used incidentally for assessment by the teacher without informing the child, then it might well give different results from an explicit test set as such. Clearly, incidental assessment can be done by the teacher as often as he wishes or his custom dictates; but the frequency of an explicit testing programme needs to be decided carefully. Here again, the attitude of working only if there is a test coming up is less common among primary children, but they will also feel that too frequent tests are a strain or a record of failure. Those who succeed are less in need of the stimulus of success, those who fail have their motivation depressed.

6. *Attitude testing*   A teacher will, almost necessarily, know something about a child's attitude to work and life, his initiative, his perserverance, his interests, his character in general. He will certainly wish to use this knowledge in making decisions about a child's progress or future programme.

   It is possible, however, that he may wish to make a deliberate assessment of the attitude, either of an individual or of the class as a whole. This could be done by creating a situation in which the response elicited can be assessed, however roughly, (e.g. 'Do as many as you like of the examples on the card') or, if for any reason a more objective assessment is needed, by using the standard attitude tests. These, it must be admitted, have a very doubtful value as far as progress in mathematics is concerned. Even when they give consistent results, it is difficult to see what the results indicate in any given set of conditions.

7. *Assessment and creativity*   The creative mathematician, like the writer, the scientist, the engineer, or anyone else who pushes forward the frontiers of human feeling, skill or knowledge, is doing something that cannot be measured numerically even if it is subject to value judgement. Much of the dispute surrounding formal assessment is the extent to which the process by-passes altogether the qualities that will make the schoolboy of today into the eminence of the future. Nevertheless, one does feel that the teacher can choose situations in which unusual abilities can begin to show themselves, usually a response to open-ended questions in which she herself can easily get out of her depth. Whether the subjective impression of potential that one gets from the work of some children is assessment in any sense, it clearly influences the teacher's final opinion and we must accept its existence.

As a conclusion, we suggest that few of us concerned with education have thought sufficiently deeply about the aims and the effect of assessment procedures. Much work has been done on standardizing and validating tests, but all this amounts to is that they give consistent results under consistent conditions.

In particular the validity of tests as predictors of progress or ability at later stages (as selection tests or 'A'-level results are supposed to be) has often been questioned, but no general action has been taken on the conclusions.

Finally, let us emphasize once again the *educational* function of assessment in evaluating progress and controlling the actual strategies of the classroom. We recommend that particular attention should be given to these aspects of assessment.

CHAPTER TEN

MATHEMATICS AND THE INTEGRATED DAY

10.1 The integrated day in general

The educational techniques and methods implied by the integrated day, the fundamental changes in attitudes called for, and the doubts and difficulties seen by many experienced and competent teachers, make this a sensitive matter for discussion. The teacher's traditional allegiance is to discrete subjects, and the general conviction is that of all subjects, mathematics is uniquely constructed. This suggests that only the simplest arithmetic is likely to emerge naturally from children's activities and requires us to formulate our topic with special reference to our subject.

We all need answers to questions such as the following:

1. Exactly what kinds of school organization and activity do people have in mind when they use phrases such as integrated day, topic approach, team teaching, interdisciplinary enquiry, environmental studies, and so on? Are they interchangeable among themselves, or do they differ among themselves as much as they appear to differ from a traditional timetable?
2. What is the place of mathematics in each of these?
3. Is it possible to gain an adequate and eventually a systematic knowledge of mathematics from such approaches?
4. Finally, since education continues beyond the primary stages, we must ask for our purpose: are any of the approaches valid at post primary levels, or do we have to make a fresh start in the middle or secondary school?

For our purpose, we shall take an 'integrated approach' as one which dispenses with the traditional classroom structure of timetabled subjects and substitute a programme of work or study which does not recognize subject divisions. Many schools have already taken the first big step by abandoning a fixed timetable, as far as the demands of shared equipment and accommodation allow, so that the class teacher moves from subject area to subject area as he thinks fit, but this is not an integrated day. Perhaps one could say that an integrated day is not differentiated into subject teaching periods at all.

As an example, we might find a thematic approach in which some rather general title is taken such as 'Communication' and split up after discussion into sub-titles which could be the subject of investigation by pupils working individually or in small groups. Examples of suggested sub-titles might be

> Travel in the Middle Ages
> The story of the telephone
> Writing through the ages
> Secret codes

We notice at once that mathematics does not arise naturally from the list, as work slanted towards other traditional subjects appears to do. The mention of codes has been made deliberately because it does suggest, *but only to a mathematically informed reader*, such topics as permutations, frequency distributions, encoding matrices, and the like, all of which can only be effectively developed at post-primary levels. They certainly go beyond the basic and essential stages which the primary child must somehow cover.

Ordinary subject teaching at some stage must begin with, or reach, an appropriate topic, such as the properties of triangles or life in palaeolithic times. The essential difference here is that the title chosen has become so general that its ramifications take us readily into different areas of study.

Hence the integrated day based on a topic approach can be run by a teacher in his own classroom. Team teaching and interdisciplinary enquiries (IDE) emerge as extensions of the integrated day. Presumably an IDE set-up moves freely between the disciplines, although it recognizes them by its very title. There is the suggestion that, although knowledge should not be fragmented in subjects, what emerges should nevertheless be acceptable to those who have not relinquished their separate allegiances. We have to accept that a majority, even if a diminishing majority, of teachers will in fact assess the results of integrated studies in this way, and this will be particularly so of the teachers who will take over the pupils for post-primary work.

Team teaching, in the sense that a number of teachers are working with a large group of children—a year group, perhaps—more or less enforces a procedure other than class teaching which now becomes physically impossible. It is a possible way of organizing an integrated topic or an IDE, and calls for mutual understanding and a willingness to cooperate that contrasts strongly with the teacher's traditional position of being entirely responsible for his own class. The purely physical difficulties—noise levels and the interference between activities—are so much a matter of personal tolerance that one finds it difficult to comment. Some children *like* to work in silence, but silence alone does not ensure a working atmosphere. Nor does it imply that all children must be doing the same task. We have already discussed this point in Chapter 2.

The term 'environmental studies' seems chosen to suggest that its topics are relevant to the child because they come from his environment. This has often been unfortunate. Since the child's environment is everything he comes into contact with other than himself, one may either make an arbitrary selection that reduces it to the topic studies already mentioned, or one may at the other extreme, allow the generality of the word to admit such variety into the child's work that it breaks into unconnected fragments each of only passing interest. Care is needed to steer a middle course.

One also hears it said that the work in mathematics should in fact 'arise from the environment', but our remarks in previous sections should make clear that this does not make mathematics an environmental study as such.

From now on we shall use the term integrated day, without reference to its possible organization in terms of team teaching or one teacher control. We note the dangers of a topic approach which becomes gimmicky, leads to an unbalanced curriculum, or gives rise in the end to disintegration. Against this, we recognize that an integrated day relates to the child as an individual, so that he can contribute to and draw from the corporate effort, whether or not these quotas can be seen to be subject disciplines as normally understood. We recognize too, that these approaches encourage, and indeed require, cooperation and understanding between teachers—ideally between all the teachers in all the schools through which the child will pass in his career.

Any integrated day must, however, meet the total educational needs of the child. It must be possible to make a systematic oversight of his progress. There must be careful observation and assessment of this progress along the lines designed by the teachers, accurate and adequate recording and, above all, careful planning of subsequent dependent work. There must also be what at first impression may often seem to be lacking: a programme designed to be sequential throughout the school, with records available and handed down the line. If these last two desiderata are not met, a child might gain more from a traditional curriculum competently taught. A sporadic dropping of systematic work in favour of a topic which may reflect a teacher's own inclinations or disinclination more than the educational needs of the pupils, may well be a pleasant oasis in the desert of the academic year and as such fully justified, but it is not an integrated learning situation. The integrated day, one feels, needs teachers of experience and maturity. Even so, they would find it helpful to have behind them resource centres from which information can be obtained, apparatus borrowed and where experiences can be discussed. This function might be undertaken by Colleges of Education who were prepared to make their own often generous supplies of books and equipment available, or by a thriving Teachers' Centre having a well-stocked library and an imaginative librarian.

The integrated day is open to failures different in kind from those already associated with more differentiated methods. The latter may take a child through a topic and leave him with a complete lack of the understanding that he needed; the integrated day if not carefully planned and sensitively supervised, may leave large gaps in knowledge, may leave essential concepts unformed, and may fail to achieve any sort of progression. Where facility depends on practice, it may well hinder progress through failure to provide it. On the other hand, the integrated day could provide just that free atmosphere and stimulating situation in which children best thrive.

10.2   The Special Problems of Mathematics

Failures are, one feels, more likely to occur in the development of mathematical knowledge because of its very nature as a progression of concepts and processes, distorted though this progression may be in modern approaches. One can find out, adequately enough, what domestic life was like a century ago without first investigating life a hundred years earlier, even if the development through the century is then less clear and significant, but one cannot master the process of division without first being familiar with multiplication.

One does not doubt that many topics are rich enough in mathematical ideas to meet the needs of the primary child. Many topics could indeed generate mathematics if only the teacher were sufficiently aware of the possibilities. What we are asking for is an eventual increase in the numbers of teachers with some specialist interest in mathematics.

It does not seem to be true that all possible investigations imply work rich enough to contain adequate mathematics. Even where number work is readily available one feels that the quantitative is frequently forced into the situation rather than abstracted from it. For a topic to be successful in developing quantitative skills and knowledge it must

1. contain situations from which mathematics may be drawn and subsequently developed;
2. contain situations to which mathematics already known may be applied;
3. require or give rise to mathematics at the appropriate level of development.

A topic which does not meet both (3) and either (1) or (2) is, however valuable to the child in other ways, of very little use in his *mathematical* development. If such a topic is pursued for other reasons, it would need to be followed by one richer in mathematical potential.

It could be that an ingenious and industrious person, with a wide general knowledge and a secure foundation of mathematics, might devise a sequence of interesting topics from which a systematic and connected programme of primary mathematics could be drawn. One wonders how the list would appeal to all the other parties in the school, whose main interest was something other than mathematics.

A reasonable conclusion would be that a teacher, happy and secure in his own mathematics, could devise some topics meeting the precise requirements already listed, and that an integrated day, however organized, could certainly give rise to suitable quantitative work; but because of the exceptional position of mathematics in education we do not consider that specific learning work in the subject can be avoided completely.

We do recommend that, even in those fortunate and progressive schools where an integrated programme is running smoothly and happily, there should be time set aside for specific work in mathematics. This would, in fact, have four main objectives:—

1. To practise skills that have emerged from or have been required by the work of any project.
2. To fill up the gaps in knowledge that must inevitably occur in situations that have not been specifically planned to yield a connected account of a mathematical topic.
3. Reconsider the mathematical work that has been done in a suitable sequence, either logical or pedagogic, so that the child can grasp its development.
4. Extend the work mathematically, adding in topics that have *not* emerged from the given project or situations so that the knowledge becomes systematic. Until it becomes systematic it is not mathematics.

Given this supplementary work, made essential by the nature of mathematics, we feel that all teachers concerned should make every effort to fit in with an integrated day planned to give rise to a reasonable proportion of quantitative studies.

We would add that the need for the child to develop individually at his own pace is no less in the middle and the secondary school, and in these schools too, integrated methods might in the end prove more appropriate than class teaching. There is certainly a case for team teaching and topic work. But the need for abstract study, and the readiness of some children at least for more academic approaches, must be borne in mind from the middle school onwards. A rather loose integrated approach could possibly lead to stagnation or even regression at secondary level. Those children who can reach, and enjoy reaching, high standards in subject-orientated studies, should be given the opportunity and be encouraged to go on.

For the average pupil at middle or lower secondary levels whose work has been 'traditionally' organized (the word is used here descriptively) it could well be that a change of approach is more important than new matter with the old approach. A year or two of integrated studies might give him a new chance, and could certainly seem more relevant to him at this stage in his life. We feel that all secondary schools, in spite of the difficulties, might consider a less structured timetable and benefit from the helical approach, as discussed in Chapter 2, in a freer atmosphere.

Appendix to report

Professional courses in primary mathematics

The teaching of mathematics has for some years been an area of sensitivity in both School and College curricula. This was highlighted in 1968 by the publication of the Dainton and Swann reports and by the criticism that followed, much of which has been directed at professional work in Colleges of Education as it is done at the time of writing. There is a strong feeling that the young teachers we are sending out are unable to meet the challenge of the new approaches and are, moreover, less able to cope with the traditional, more formal methods. We admit some truth in the charge, yet the problems faced are immense. Of students admitted to the Colleges in 1968, 27·5 per cent of the men and 44·6 per cent of the women lacked even the elementary qualification of 'O'-level mathematics. But no statistics can show the sheer lack of mathematical understanding or the incidence of dislike and even fear.

The A.T.C.D.E. Mathematics Section decided to approach this problem, first by collecting opinions and criticism from groups of teachers known to the investigators. The survey was not comprehensive nor statistically analysed, but it had the advantage of collecting opinions from teachers in contact with their local Colleges who were aware of the problems involved.

It is inevitable that much of the criticism referred to a situation that will inevitably change in some way as a result of the James Report, and has no direct relevance to a programme which could be based on some form of consecutive training, perhaps with a full involvement of experienced teachers at a suitable stage in the cycle. Yet many of the old problems will remain with us; we must learn and learn well from past events.

We also found that the desirable attributes and skills of a young entrant to the profession as listed by his colleagues read more like an idealized manifesto for the profession rather than a practical set of qualifications for an individual. The demands made of the young entrant's mathematical competence and knowledge seemed overwhelming in view of his role as a general educator of the primary child. They were paralleled by a further all-embracing demand that he should be able to organize all kinds of working methods with all ages and abilities according to the school in which he found himself, feeling at home among backward children, open plan schools, family grouping, teaching teams, initial reading schemes, curriculum development, and indeed all aspects of primary education. It seemed clear that only a teacher of experience and maturity could begin to shape up to the standards set by groups of his colleagues, and then only in those fields where his own interests finally came to take shape.

We feel that the proposals of the James Report, which leaves the second 'professional' cycle open-ended, with extensive provision for a third cycle of in-service study, could certainly help to move the situation nearer to the teachers' own ideals.

The A.T.C.D.E. also mounted a second prong attack on the problem at the 1970 Homerton Conference. Although the basic theme of the sessions was 'Progression in Primary Mathematics' as covered in the earlier chapters of this report, a working party devoted some time to what we might call a practical idealized syllabus of professional study. It is practical in the sense that it contains not only what we think is necessary but what can be done with non-specialists in mathematics; but it is idealized in that even under the James proposals there may be difficulty in finding a due allowance of time. We felt that any discussion of primary mathematics is incomplete without reference to the appropriate knowledge and skills of those who teach it, and we offer the syllabus that follows for the consideration of all concerned. It is a common core syllabus aimed at the entire primary range of work. We do not claim that every young teacher should be able to swing into work at every level, but that the sections should be given each its own emphasis as needed. The syllabus, offered as it is to the general teacher, can scarcely be given adequate treatment either during the present three-year courses at colleges or during the proposed Second Cycle. Once again, a powerful and effective Third Cycle programme is probably our best hope for the future of primary mathematics.

A syllabus for professional studies in mathematics

Note: *Any technical terms used in the sections which follow are for the information of those planning the courses. As far as possible a teacher should, we feel, master the vocabulary of the subject taught, but that of mathematics is so specialized and inappropriate to ordinary discourse that we must leave it to the judgement of those in the classrooms to decide in what language to express the concepts being taught.*

1. *The nature and use of mathematics*
   Every opportunity should be taken to give mathematics its special and intellectual setting. Each topic of the course should be seen against a background of meaning and use.
2. *The language of mathematics*
   The ideas and vocabulary of sets, relations, and mappings at an elementary level. The universal set, the null set, sub-sets, disjoint sets, complements, unions, and intersections, illustrated by concrete materials, Venn diagrams, punched cards. Symbolic representation. Relations within a set and their properties. Well ordering and partial ordering relations. Equivalence and the concept of equivalence classes.
   Relations between elements of two sets
   many : many, many : 1, 1 : many, and 1 : 1 correspondences
   Ordered pairs and cartesian products
   Mappings. Into and onto mappings

3. *The concept of number and operations with number*
   The use of the language of mathematics to clarify the concept of number
   Cardinal and ordinal number
   Counting as correspondence
   Number bonds as mappings
   Operations with sets leading to the concept of isomorphism
   The four rules and their relations as operation and inverse
   The formal laws of operations—commutativity, associativity and the distributive law
   The four rules as operations with sets
   Place value and bases of notation
   Number patterns arising from the notation

4. *Early work with number in the classroom*
   The approach to number in the infant classroom
   The process of counting and learning of the numerals
   Use of appropriate apparatus
   Schemes of number work
   Teaching the operations
   The use of structured and extemporized apparatus, textbooks and work cards.
   The interpretation of symbols (e.g. is 2 × 3 to be taken as 2 lots of 3 or 3 lots of 2?)
   Notation and place value
   The use of number patterns
   Number games suitable for class use

5. *Computation in the classroom*
   The four rules and the relations between them given by the scheme

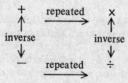

   Examples of the processes of arithmetic in their various aspects (e.g. division as sharing and grouping, multiplication as magnification or repeated addition) and acquaintance with all methods of calculation commonly found (e.g. subtraction by decomposition or equal addition)

6. *The extension of number work*
   The use of number line and other apparatus to introduce rationals and signed integers

7. *Graphical methods in the classroom*
   Arrow diagrams
   Early work in graphical representation leading to the use of isotypes and symbols
   Types of chart

Introduction of axes and scales
Venn diagrams and mappings between sets
Introduction to functional relationships
The reading and interpretation of graphs
Interpolation and its validity
Correct use of word 'histogram'

8. *Ratio and proportion*
   The concept of ratio and the equivalence of fractions
   Ratio as a linear relationship
   Speed, density and other ratios involving measure
   Trigonometry and its treatment at primary level
   The use of tables and ready reckoners

9. *Measure (at student level)*
   Familiarity with the SI units of length, mass, and temperature on the Celsius scale, of the derived units of area and volume, and the usual knowledge of time and angle
   At this transitional stage one should be able to discuss and initiate work using metric units
   The limitations of measure
   Limits and accuracy of measurement. Tolerance
   Estimation and approximation
   Contrast of continuous and discontinuous quantities (e.g. money as a measure of value)
   The distinction between mass and weight

10. *Measure in the classroom*
    The general development of the child's concepts. What can and what cannot be measured.
    One measure (length is probably the most suitable) should be treated in detail with progression of concepts and activities from reception to middle school level
    Discussion of extension of the principles established to the other measures of capacity, mass, area, volume, temperature, and measure of speed, density, and so on as appropriate

11. *Special techniques implied by measure*
    Exemplified by work in area, which involves:—
    Tessellations
    Improvised units for irregular areas
    The rectangle and triangle as special cases
    The shape of the unit
    The child's confusion of perimeter and area
    A similar treatment for volume and its connection with capacity

12. *Time*
    The concept of time as continuous and as a set of arbitrary points on a scale
    Historical background of time measurement, with reasons for the natural and

the man-made units
Teaching the twenty-four hour clock
Timetables
The calendar and its patterns
Pendulums, water clocks, sand-glasses, rolling ball timers, etc.

13. *Money*

Comprehensive classroom work on use of coins, recording of prices, giving change, construction of ready reckoners
Organization of classroom shops

14. *Number in action*

Finding or constructing practical problems suitable for class use involving measures and money, with graphical representation where appropriate

15. *Spatial concepts as an informal treatment at student level*

(a)   The concepts of topology—boundaries, regions, interior points, networks, continuous deformations, with the concept of 'invariant'
(b)   Metrical concepts—names and simple properties of plane and solid configurations
Convex and concave sets
Similarity and projection
Congruence
The isometries of the plane informally treated
Descriptive symmetry
Patterns produced by symmetrical units
Tessellation of plane surfaces
Curves and curve tracing
Introduction to motion geometry
Rotation and circulation
Angle, its definition and measure
The concept of a vector

16. *Statistics*

Tabulation of information
The uses and misuses of statistics
Elementary ideas of probability
Descriptive account of mean, mode, and median
Simple ideas of dispersion
Scatter diagrams and the ideas of correlation and ranking
Marking systems

This list of topics covers a proposed core of professional knowledge which is specifically *mathematical*, although it attempts to place mathematics in its social, psychological, and scientific context and to relate it to other aspects of children's learning. We feel that the simple utilitarian aspect of mathematics, so relevant to elementary mathematical learning in the past, does not by itself justify the large amount of time spent on the subject in primary schools. Rather is mathematics to be seen as a fundamental and growing part of our technological society, a vital element in the general education of any school child, and a study having aesthetic appeal in its own right. The emphasis in the classroom has moved from rule learning and application to investigation and problem solving, from single solution questions to the use of an open ended situation, from teacher-dominated to group-organized classrooms. Against this background our syllabus suggests a necessary content.

We conclude on a note of cautious optimism. The James proposals, however modified or implemented, cannot simply be ignored; they imply a big change in professional preparation. It may not be clear what the actual pattern of training will be, so that we do not at this stage make any suggestions about how or when our syllabus should be operated. We offer it to the profession as our ideal of the mathematical equipment of the general practitioner in primary education, and hope that world enough and time can be found to develop it.